HOME & GARDEN TELEVISION

DESIGN ON A DIME

MEREDITH® BOOKS
DES MOINES, IOWA

DESIGN ON A DIME

Editor: Amy Tincher-Durik
Senior Associate Design Director: Ken Carlson
Copy Chief: Terri Fredrickson
Copy and Production Editor: Victoria Forlini
Editorial Operations Manager: Karen Schirm
Managers, Book Production: Pam Kvitne, Marjorie J. Schenkelberg, Rick von Holdt
Contributing Writer: Paula Marshall
Contributing Editor: Cathy Kramer, Cathy Kramer Design
Contributing Copy Editor: Jane Woychick
Contributing Proofreaders: Dan Degen, Beth Havey, Juliet Jacobs
Contributing Photographers: Michael Garland, Tommy Miyasaki
Photo Stylist: Robin Tucker
Indexer: Elizabeth Parson
Illustrations: Michael Bentley
Editorial and Design Assistants: Kaye Chabot, Karen McFadden, Mary Lee Gavin

Meredith® Books
Editor in Chief: Linda Raglan Cunningham
Design Director: Matt Strelecki
Executive Editor, Home Decorating and Design: Denise L. Caringer

Publisher: James D. Blume
Executive Director, Marketing: Jeffrey Myers
Executive Director, New Business Development: Todd M. Davis
Executive Director, Sales: Ken Zagor
Director, Operations: George A. Susral
Director, Production: Douglas M. Johnston
Business Director: Jim Leonard

Vice President and General Manager: Douglas J. Guendel

Meredith Publishing Group
President, Publishing Group: Stephen M. Lacy
Vice President-Publishing Director: Bob Mate

Meredith Corporation
Chairman and Chief Executive Officer: William T. Kerr

In Memoriam: E. T. Meredith III (1933-2003)

All of us at Meredith® Books are dedicated to providing you with information and ideas to enhance your home. We welcome your comments and suggestions. Write to us at: Meredith Books, Home Decorating and Design Editorial Department, 1716 Locust St., Des Moines, IA 50309-3023.

If you would like to purchase any of our home decorating and design, cooking, crafts, gardening, or home improvement books, check wherever quality books are sold. Or visit us at: meredithbooks.com

Cover Photograph: Michael Garland

CONTENTS

GETTING TO KNOW THE TEAMS

Lee Snijders

Lee Snijders's approach to design comes from his diverse creative background: During his tenure as a Walt Disney Imagineer, he learned that as long as you have imagination, your creativity is limitless. He has taken this lesson into his own business, Lee Snijders Designs; his sophisticated interiors range from classic midcentury modern to daring tropical styles. *Design on a Dime* allows Lee to combine his experience in entertainment and his love of interior design.

Summer Baltzer

Summer Baltzer began her decorating and design career more than a decade ago, working for community theater productions in the Southern California area and running her own residential interior design business. She received her formal training at California State University-Northridge in the family environmental sciences department, where she studied architectural and interior design. Summer has designed interiors to suit all budgets, but she loves the challenge of designing a room on a dime.

Charles Burbridge

Los Angeles native Charles Burbridge left his growing decorative painting and interiors business to join the HGTV family. He has been a working actor for the past decade and is a founding member of an improvisational sketch comedy troupe. Dividing his time between his creative pursuits has always been a challenge, but he has found the perfect blending of his many interests and artistic abilities as part of the *Design on a Dime* team.

Kristan Cunningham

Hailing from West Virginia, Kristan Cunningham studied interior design at the University of Charleston. In 1997 she moved to Los Angeles and joined a small edgy firm, which gave her the opportunity to explore the structural and technical sides of design. As host and designer on *Design on a Dime*, Kristan relishes the chance to "get back to the basics" and share her fresh approach to budget-conscious design.

Spencer Anderson

Spencer Anderson grew up in Houston where he studied art and metal sculpture. At Florida State University, he continued to sculpt but found a new interest in designing sets and building props for his friends' movies. After graduating with a bachelor's degree in fine arts, he moved to Los Angeles and became an assistant art director on small cable films. Spencer's artistic background and talent for building are a perfect combination for *Design on a Dime*—and unlike his movie props, the pieces aren't destroyed after the show ends!

Dave Sheinkopf

For Dave Sheinkopf, growing up in New York City was a breeding ground for creativity. At a young age he found himself in the spotlight, working on big and small screens as an actor. After years of focusing his talents on television and film, Dave discovered a love of building and designing. *Design on a Dime* feeds his creative side, allowing him to blend his talents in acting and furniture building.

IT'S YOUR DIME, (SO) SPEND IT WISELY

Since its debut HGTV's series *Design on a Dime* has become a trusted destination for viewers who want savvy design ideas for little financial investment. Week after week, designers Sam Kivett, Lee Snijders, and Kristan Cunningham—along with design coordinators Summer Baltzer, Charles Burbridge, Dave Sheinkopf, and Spencer Anderson—introduce viewers to home-owners who want to give a problem room a new look and increased functionality. The bedrooms, living rooms, kitchens, home offices, and other rooms they tackle suffer from various ailments, from a lack of storage to a lack of style. With a

$1,000 budget, 24 hours, and lots of design tricks, the teams pull together stylish solutions that have attracted many fans, not to mention happy homeowners. Viewers enjoy the drama—will the teams complete all the projects in time, and will the homeowners love their newly transformed rooms? However, *Design on a Dime* is much more than great tel-evision. The show presents a philosophy of mak-ing smart choices when planning to redecorate any room of the home; each episode proves that creating a stylish home requires imagina-tion, not big money. That's also the goal of this book: It's designed to show you how you can adapt the solid design principles, projects, and tried-and-true techniques you see on the pro-gram to make your own decorating dreams a reality.

Are you living in your first apartment with only hand-me-downs to fill the space? You'll find tips to help you pull your style together. Is your dated kitchen in need of new lighting and fresh color? You'll get innovative ideas to help jump-start your creativity. In these pages you'll find 21

rooms featured on *Design on a Dime*—as well as special features on topics such as painting and creating focal points. You'll also get helpful hints from the designers themselves and you'll soon discover that a small budget can yield a big payoff!

This Book Is a Road Map

This book is divided into four sections: Rearrange, Recolor, Remake, and Restyle; these are the four basic steps to designing on a dime.

Each section includes inspiring room makeovers, and each makeover combines the four steps in a winning design.

In **Rearrange** you'll discover that function and looks both stem from thoughtful room arrangement. This section proves that strategic furniture placement can effectively redefine a space.

The rooms in **Recolor** show the power of paint and fabric—two of the easiest and least expensive ways to add pizzazz to a room. Fresh paint colors—from neutrals to eye-popping jewel tones—and stylish yet practical pillows and window treatments give the spaces featured new life.

Reusing an existing piece of furniture is more cost-effective than purchasing a brand-new one. Sometimes customizing a thrift store chair or revitalizing a hand-me-down table is the simplest way to bring style into your living spaces, and it is certainly rewarding to do the job yourself. That's what **Remake** is all about: You'll discover how easy it is to add a crackle finish to a tired nightstand and you'll learn how to turn an ordinary dining room table into a place for children to nurture their artistic abilities.

After you've identified the ways to rearrange, recolor, and remake your room, it's time to focus on the small things—the accents and accessories that have lots of impact. In **Restyle** you'll see how these little details can bring your personal style to life.

To complete this book of amazing transformations, a room arranging kit is included, along with a comprehensive section devoted to resources. The arranging kit will teach you how to create a space that functions the way you need it to. Use it to help you picture how your room will function with different arrangements; after you perfect the plan on paper, move the actual furniture into place. Floor plan ideas are

included to help you design the room of your dreams. Finally, the resources section is a user-friendly guide to help you find the materials featured in each makeover.

Before viewing the makeovers, read through the basic guidelines that follow. They'll help you understand what makes the *Design on a Dime* philosophy work. Then you'll be able to approach all your decorating dilemmas with a clearer sense of the end goal— and how to get there on a budget without sacrificing style or functionality.

Think About What You Have and Need

Whenever you begin the redecorating process, it's important to look at the key pieces you already have—furnishings, accessories, artwork—and the features of the room itself.

Is your sofa exactly the right size and scale for your living room? Keep it! If the color or pattern doesn't exactly match the new overall look you desire, dress the piece with an inexpensive slipcover or pillows. Has your

dinette set seen better days? Imagine how you might be able to update its look with a fresh coat of paint—or even a treatment of linseed oil—and new drop-in seats for the chairs.

That said, one of the keys to making over a room is knowing when it's time to let go and invest in new pieces. If your recliner has a sagging seat, damaged upholstery, and a broken reclining mechanism, it may be destined for the trash heap rather than your newly styled room.

Once you've determined what pieces are worth keeping—and what to toss—consider what you need to pull the look together. Do you require storage in your living room? Consider an armoire or console that has closed areas to conceal clutter. Are you eating dinner

on the floor because you don't have a proper table and chairs? Add that to your list.

Look at the room itself and note its basic elements: the architecture (is your room a plain box, void of molding?), flooring (is the hardwood floor worth refinishing, or do you need new carpeting?), and high-ticket items such as cabinets. These are all things you can change if you want to dedicate your time and financial resources to them; however, if you merely want to bring in fresh color and decorative touches, the investment is minimal in comparison. This book focuses on the latter—redecorating—not more-costly, time-consuming remodeling.

Finally, when evaluating what you have and what your needs are, remember the main reason for the makeover. Has your new baby's

Select a Theme Based on What You Love

Do some of your existing furnishings lend themselves to a particular decorating style? Is there a new style you want to try? Follow your instincts and be brave—you're about to create your own custom design!

First, look around you for inspiration: Magazines, televised decorating programs, shops, and your friends' and families' homes are rife with new ideas. After you've found the look you want to try, research the style, using books or the Internet. What colors, motifs, textures, materials, and furnishings best suit your chosen decorating style? Do you already have pieces that fit the look? If not, where can you find them? Keeping these details in mind will help you stay focused while you shop.

to be either. Once you determine the pieces you need immediately (for example, a suitable desk for home computing) and the pieces you can add over time (such as decorative artwork), you are on your way to making smart decisions. On *Design on a Dime*, the teams have $1,000 to make over a room. This is a great starting point to see what you can do with a set amount of money. However, only you know what you can really afford: Maybe it's $100, $500, or $5,000.

When figuring out your budget, consider the price range of a typical item. For instance, a brand-new quality sofa can cost many hundreds to even thousands of dollars, which might consume your entire budget. However, many great pieces are available at secondhand and resale shops. If you find such a piece, calculate the

Keeping your big-picture goals in mind will bring the plan into focus and help you design a room that functions perfectly for you.

nursery taken over your dedicated office space, forcing you to look for desk space elsewhere in the house? Are you newly married and uncertain about how to combine two people's possessions in one space? Keeping your big-picture goals in mind will bring the plan into focus and help you design a room that functions perfectly.

However, no matter what style you choose, keep your mind and eyes open. Watch for interesting pieces that complement rather than match your overall style. For instance, if you love contemporary design, mix in some traditional pieces that have shapes, lines, or colors that echo your contemporary pieces. By doing so you'll create a space that's original and interesting, custom-designed for your tastes.

Determine a Budget

After you decide what pieces you'll reuse and what pieces you need, it's time to consider what you can afford. The key here is to prioritize; Rome wasn't built in a day, and your room doesn't have

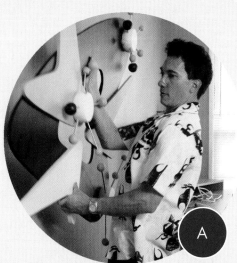

A Lee hangs a piece of custom artwork. **B** The tried-and-true decorating principles that the two *Design on a Dime* teams execute in every episode work away from home too: Lee, Summer, and Charles tackled a dorm room shared by two young men. See page 166 for more on this room.

A

cost of transforming it and add the sum to the price tag (new cushions and upholstery can be pricey if done by a professional).

Finally, budget necessary tools and supplies. Paintbrushes and paint, nails and screws, and window treatment hardware are a few of the items you may need to make over your room. If you don't have all these items already and you

waiting to be found in thrift stores, secondhand stores, discount stores, and even your very own attic or garage (remember that table you've been planning to refinish?). Follow these cues for choosing furniture and fabric when you shop:

Shopping for Furniture

Whenever you're shopping for furniture, keep the following pointers in mind:
- Think scale and proportion of the furnishings in relation to each other and to the room to ensure all pieces appear compatible. For example, even if they suit the same decorating style, a slender chair standing next to a hefty overstuffed sofa will look out of place. Similarly, small furnishings—unless grouped—will get lost when placed in a large room.
- Look for reproduction pieces. For example, if you love pieces from the 1950s, you may consider a vintage chrome dinette set. Unfortunately, these pieces can be quite pricey; sets in great

cleaned with professional or do-it-yourself foam or steam cleaners, but figure this into the overall cost of the piece.

Shopping for Fabric

When purchasing fabric, first consider its end use: Will it be a slipcover in a room that's used by children? If so, choose a heavy, sturdy fabric such as corduroy or denim. A gauzy fabric could make a breezy window treatment for a cottage-style space. After deciding on the general type of fabric you need, follow these tips:

If you love contemporary design, mix in some traditional pieces that have shapes, lines, and colors that echo your contemporary pieces.

can't afford to buy them, borrow them from friends and family members. Consider renting high-ticket items such as saws and air compressors rather than purchasing them.

Go Shopping

Although shopping for new items to fill your space can be a daunting task—because you will be faced with myriad choices in all price ranges—it can also be great fun! Treasures are

condition cost about $1,000. However, many high-quality reproduction sets are available, and they're much less expensive.
- If you can't find exactly what you want, look at pieces in new ways. For instance, a stool can make a charming bedside table, and a bookcase turned upside down can act as a low coffee table (add wheels to the bottom and it's mobile).
- At secondhand stores look for furnishings in good condition that won't require major repair. Although sagging cushions can be replaced and worn upholstery can be dressed with a slipcover, it's essential to weigh the cost of these repairs against the longevity of the piece. Look for stains and pay attention to strong odors on upholstered pieces. Many pieces can be

A This dining room was formerly a long boxy space with a great dining set but no real style—until Kristan, Dave, and Spencer came along. Now, gray paint and planter boxes create a focal point on one wall, custom lights hang above the table, and new drop-in seats and slipcovers impart a tailored look. See page 72 for more on this room. **B** Summer prepares to complete a 1950s atomic-style light fixture.

See page 72 for more on this room.

Before You Head Out the Door

For your next shopping expedition, keep the following in mind:
- Take a shopping list with you to keep yourself focused. If you happen to see the perfect lamp to complement your overall look, grab it. Then get back to your list and the goal you set out to accomplish.
- If you are shopping for furniture, measure your door openings, stair widths, landings, and other key spots; you don't want to purchase what you think is the perfect piece only to find that it won't fit into your house. Then, take a tape measure along to measure furnishings.
- Avoid temptation—incredible bargains that don't fit your overall plan aren't really bargains. If that great buy isn't in the style you need, leave it at the store.
- Take fabric swatches and paint chips along to ensure a good color match.
- Plan your day: If you plan to shop garage sales, head out bright and early to get the best pieces. Also, for garage sales and secondhand stores, bring cash; you'll have a hard time charging your purchases! If you plan to spend your day at a flea market, take water, packing materials (for breakables), and sturdy bags or backpacks. Finally, wear comfortable clothing and shoes.

● Take accurate measurements before you leave the house. For example, measure the width and length of a window prior to purchasing fabric for a window treatment.

● To take the guesswork out of mixing patterns, look for coordinated groupings.

● Buy extra, especially if you find the fabric on a discount table; you may need only 1 yard now, but if you later decide to make throw pillows or need more fabric to complete the project, you'll be prepared. Extra fabric also allows you to match up the pattern on a large project, such as floor-length curtain panels or a duvet cover.

Pulling It All Together

Now that you've gathered all your supplies, purchased furnishings and accessories, and determined what do-it-yourself projects you'd like to tackle, prioritize your projects. If you are painting, make that your first job; paint splatters could ruin that new sofa. Next, plan the furniture arrangement; this will lead you to choose suitable places for such elements as lighting.

The two teams on *Design on a Dime* completely overhaul a room in a day; let your room evolve over time instead. Choose a few key pieces to start the makeover and keep your end

Rome wasn't built in a day, and your room doesn't have to be either. Once you determine the pieces you need immediately and the pieces you can add over time, you are on your way to making smart decisions.

Tips from the *Design on a Dime* Cast

The hosts and design coordinators on *Design on a Dime* have many great strategies for nearly any decorating dilemma:

● Need a quick pick-me-up for your newly redecorated space? Lee Snijders believes you can warm up any space with nature's accessory: plants. The free-flowing lines and fresh colors soften the hard edges of furnishings.

● Kristan Cunningham offers this technique for creating a unique focal point: Group favorite items or collections. For example, arranging candles, pitchers, or glassware of varying heights and shapes—but in one consistent color—against a solid-color surface, such as a wall or bookcase, can make the grouping command attention and usher in contemporary flair.

● Do you have a small room but big ideas? Spencer Anderson says: Shear airy curtains let in more light than those made of heavy opaque fabrics; the increase in light will help to visually expand the room. If you have few windows, harness the reflective power of mirrors to make it appear larger.

● Be mindful of any special requirements a specific fabric may have. For instance, heavy fabrics, such as denim, require a specialty needle for a sewing machine, while lightweight fabrics, such as silk, may need to be stabilized for ease of stitching. If you are unsure, consult an associate at the store before you buy.

● Care of fabric is another consideration: Some fabrics may already be pretreated for stain resistance, while others can be treated with spray-on stain repellents available at fabric and furniture stores. Some fabrics, such as heavier weight fabrics used for tight-fitting slipcovers that are left in place, can be carefully vacuumed with a soft-bristle attachment (just ensure loose items like buttons are secure).

———————————————————

Ⓐ Kristan attaches feather trim to a lampshade for a flashy Vegas-style bedroom. Ⓑ An anxious homeowner opens his eyes on Lee's cue to see his newly transformed living room. Ⓒ Kristan, Dave, and Spencer turned a once-drab guest room into this sleek contemporary space, complete with a stunning padded headboard that acts as a striking focal point. See page 172 for more on this room.

decorating goal in mind as you gradually add new furnishings and accessories to your room.

Let's Decorate!

Are you ready to start your decorating journey? Sit back, relax, and get inspiration from the 21 fabulous rooms designed and executed by the talented *Design on a Dime* teams. You may be surprised how inexpensive great design can be.

REARRANGE YOUR ROOMS

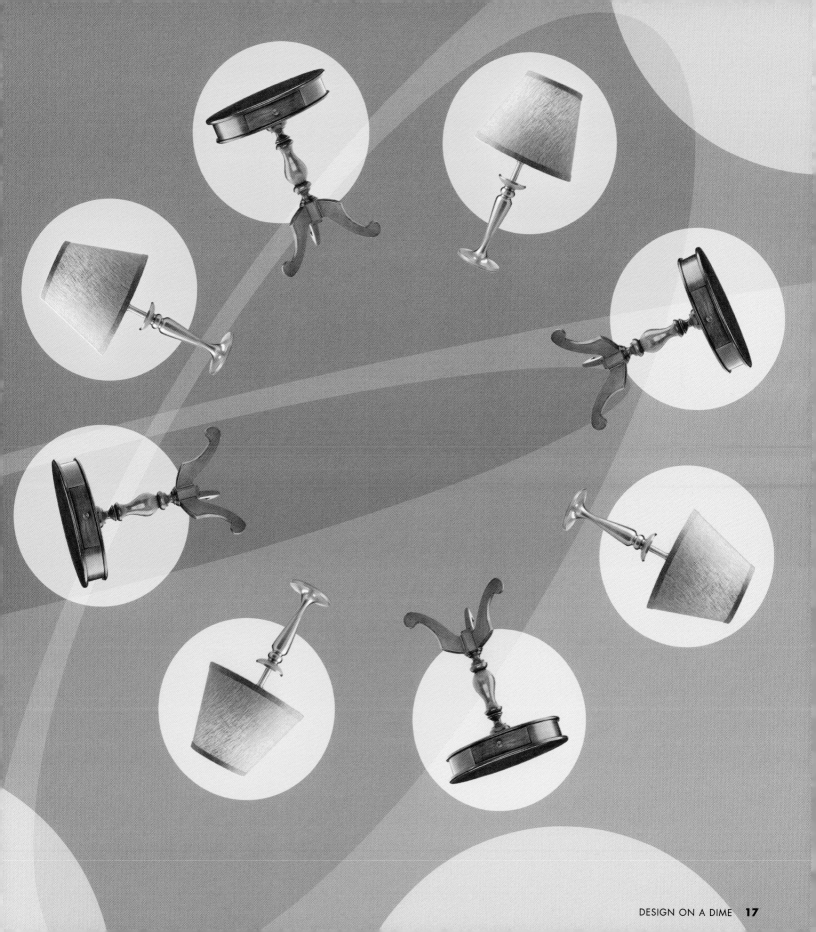

MAKE IT MODERN

Large rooms can be a mixed blessing: Although they provide ample space for multiple people and activities, this spaciousness can be overwhelming, especially if you don't have adequate furnishings to fill the room—and you aren't sure how to arrange what you do have for maximum functionality. Such was the case in this room. Used for entertaining, dining, and home computing, the uninspired space lacked appropriate pieces to serve each activity. If you are faced with a similar dilemma, study this makeover for ideas on how to infuse a multipurpose room with real purpose—and style.

Design Team

Lee Snijders, Summer Baltzer, Charles Burbridge

The Situation

• This large, sparsely furnished, all-white space in an apartment serves as a living room/office/dining area.

• The vertical blinds are worn and the other windows are left bare.

• The homeowner desires a clean, uncluttered room that functions well and showcases his love of fish and aquariums.

The Solutions

• Using smart arranging strategies, the team creates distinct areas within the room that allow for TV viewing, dining, and office use. And it brings in color by painting the walls a pale but rich brown—a neutral color that can easily be painted over when the homeowner moves.

• Contemporary touches are used to enliven the windows: The blinds are painted silver and reversible window treatment panels provide privacy and bold color.

• The new look is sleek and minimalist, complete with streamlined accessories and small fishbowls.

A Place to Entertain and Relax

This room needs to function in three ways, so the layout has to maximize space while reducing clutter. Despite this challenge, the versatile new arrangement leaves plenty of open floor space and still offers flexibility.

Previously, this room offered only a sofa and a small side table for entertaining and relaxing. Positioned next to a high window and quite far from the TV, the sofa provided seating for two at most; others had to sit on the floor to enjoy a meal or entertainment. Because the existing sofa is comfortable and has a strong color—blue with crisp white piping—it remains in the room, in nearly the same position as before. However, to fill the large void between the sofa and TV, a coffee table (previously used as a desk) is moved into place, where it serves up snacks for TV viewers.

(A) New storage pieces and three-dimensional artwork on the walls bring focus to this once-cluttered space. (B) Positioned behind the sofa, the homeowner's large aquarium now has a prominent spot in the room. (C) New pillows with bold blocks of beige, blue, and white bring comfort and style into the room.

A

B

Ottomans are positioned near the sofa to bring more seating into the mix. They can easily be moved around the room to suit seating needs, and their flat tops make them suitable for use as makeshift side tables.

To bring attention to the homeowner's large aquarium, a console is added behind the sofa.

A Brushed-metal accents abound in this sleekly styled space. These pieces stand on a custom desk riser that's covered with graphic vinyl flooring. **B** Beta fish in small fishbowls positioned throughout the room serve as decorative elements—and highlight the homeowner's love of fish. **C** This $60 console offers practical storage space and provides an ideal spot for slim lamps that offer handy task lighting.

The piece, purchased for $60 at a secondhand furniture shop, has clean lines that fit with the contemporary style chosen for the space. The scale of the console is perfect; it stands just a bit shorter than the sofa so that the fish tank doesn't overwhelm the main seating area. The console has a laminated top that won't be damaged by water splashed from the tank. It also features closed storage space, a great place to stash stuff when company unexpectedly drops by. The console is also home to new lamps, which flank the fish tank. During the day the room gets plenty of natural light; the lamps step in at night, providing task lighting with style.

Two Ways for Apartment Dwellers to Bring Style into Their Spaces

Lee Snijders offers these great ideas for renters who want to add style to their rooms:

If you can't paint the walls, use lighting to add texture and depth to the room. For example, floor cans positioned behind potted plants create an interesting shadow effect on walls. Hung from the ceiling, can and track lights offer downlighting, taking hard edges off furnishings for a dramatic effect. Innovations in fixtures allow you to install some types without any ceiling wiring, which is perfect for apartments because renters can't typically alter the structure of a space.

Look to the floor: Area rugs conceal carpeting and offer a great way to anchor furniture groupings. If you have few furnishings, an area rug can give your room a more filled-in appearance.

A

BEFORE

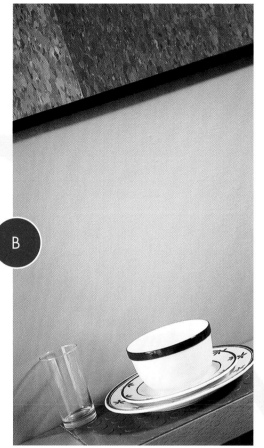

A ready-made counter, suspended from the wall, provides enough space for meals without inhabiting valuable floor space.

To visually separate the entertainment area from the dining and work spaces, a new beige chenille rug anchors the sofa, coffee table, and ottomans in the audiovisual corner.

A Place to Work

Computing on a coffee table while sitting on the floor isn't impossible, it's just uncomfortable.

Ⓐ Finding a spot for dining doesn't get easier than this: A slim shelf is mounted to the wall, eliminating the need for a freestanding table. This is a great solution when floor space is at a premium. Ⓑ Leftover pieces of vinyl flooring (from the desk project) are used as easy-to-clean place mats. Ⓒ Lee created dimensional artwork with various shapes of plywood and bendable aluminum rods. The cabinet stores CDs and the top supports three fish bowls.

The homeowner can attest to that. Now a sleek desk, made from ¾-inch plywood, ready-made brushed-metal legs, and easy-clean vinyl flooring, gets the office space off the floor. The desk faces the wall, creating an intimate work area. Now one person can work virtually undisturbed while others do various activities in other parts of the room. To make the new office area even more user-friendly, a riser, constructed of the same materials as the desk, puts the monitor at eye level, and a wipe board offers a convenient place to jot notes.

A Place to Eat

Previously the dining area was standing-room-only—unless

Color-block pillows dress up the once-bare sofa, and a clever, reversible grommet-top window treatment that can be configured in different ways adds a swath of color to the walls.

diners sat on the floor. A counter, suspended from the wall, now provides enough room for meals without inhabiting valuable floor space. Two stools in metal and black plastic offer a stylish way to enjoy a meal. They also allow guests to visit with the cook without getting in the way in the kitchen on the other side of the pass-through. Place mats created from the same vinyl flooring that graces the desk top dress up the counter. These easy-to-clean mats are a great way to use leftover material and lend a high-tech feel to the space.

Decorative Touches Pull It All Together

Before the *Design on a Dime* team transformed this room, it was devoid of style: bare walls, a single ill-placed floor lamp, and a patterned rug that didn't coordinate with the sofa. The room now exhibits the hallmarks of contemporary design: clean-lined furnishings; silver accents on the blinds, table legs, and custom wall art; and doses of bold colors in strong geometric patterns. These simple elements provide some much-needed punch.

The unattractive utilitarian blinds receive a coat of silver metallic spray paint for the look of aluminum at a fraction of the price. Only one side is painted; from the outside the blinds match those in the other apartments.

This room lacked a clear focal point; a clever combination of artwork and display space fills the void, dressing up the wall above the TV. The wall sculpture is made of plywood and malleable aluminum rods and is designed to fit around the wall-mounted storage unit. The three-dimensional piece has great visual impact and breaks up the solid wall with interesting shapes.

Color-block pillows dress up the once-bare sofa, and a clever, reversible grommet-top window treatment that can be configured in different ways adds a swath of color to the walls. Framed linoleum squares hung above the dining area introduce another splash of color.

Ⓐ Two sleek chairs—in brushed metal and heavy-duty black plastic—are the perfect companions for the slender wall-mounted shelf.
Ⓑ Light streams in through the silver-painted vertical blinds, and a plush ottoman stands at the ready to provide extra seating.

CUSTOM DESK

Ready-made furnishings can be expensive, and sometimes prefabricated pieces such as desks made of less-than-quality materials don't stand up over time. This stylish desk and coordinating riser were constructed for less than $100 with ¾-inch plywood, ready-made screw-on legs, and vinyl flooring. Black paint and gray flooring with geometric motifs grace this desk; for a custom desk choose a paint color and vinyl flooring that complement your overall decorating scheme.

Ⓒ Before the *Design on a Dime* team arrived, the homeowner sat on the floor and used a low coffee table as a desk.

C

BEFORE

For a video demonstration of this project and more *Design on a Dime* ideas, visit HGTV.com/dod

You Will Need
¾" plywood, circular saw*
4 tall screw-on table legs, 4 short table legs, hardware
Latex paint in desired finish and color, paintbrush
Vinyl flooring in the desired color and pattern
Sandpaper, tack cloth
Screwdriver
Flooring adhesive, putty knife, utility knife, brayer, tape measure
Cloth or sponge
***If you don't have a saw to cut the plywood to the desired size, have the wood cut at the lumberyard or home improvement center; often, simple cuts are made free of charge.**

1 Cut the plywood to the desired size for the desk top. Cut a smaller piece of plywood for the desk riser. Sand each piece and wipe away any dust with the tack cloth. Paint the bottom and edges of each cut plywood piece; let dry.

2 Attach the tall table legs to the bottom of the desk (Photo A). Attach the short legs to the riser.

3 Cut a piece of vinyl flooring to the dimensions of the desk top. Using the putty knife, spread an even layer of flooring adhesive onto the desk top. Starting at one corner, carefully set the vinyl flooring on the desk top. Smooth the vinyl onto the surface, using a brayer to ensure the flooring adheres to the surface. Wipe up any adhesive that seeps from beneath the flooring, using a damp cloth or sponge. Repeat the procedure with a smaller piece of vinyl flooring for the riser (Photos B and C).

A

B

C

A

BEFORE

DISORDERLY (TO) DYNAMIC

Do you often work out of your home? Are you fortunate enough to have a space to dedicate solely to a home office? If you're working in a corner of a borrowed room instead, take cues from this makeover. This space is divided into areas that function well and feel roomy; a movable divider wall that conceals unsightly clutter is the key to success in this office located in a lovely cottage-style garage.

Design Team

Sam Kivett, Summer Baltzer, Charles Burbridge

The Situation

• This wide-open space is unorganized and it doesn't serve any function well. The lack of color and style adds to the problem.

• The lighting is insufficient for an office space.

• Windows let in light and views of the lush garden outside. However, with no window treatments, privacy is compromised.

• The exposed storage is disorderly.

The Solutions

• The space is reconfigured to allow for separate meeting, office, and storage space. A movable divider wall helps define the areas. Contemporary materials such as corrugated metal and burlap move in and combine with bold color and streamlined furnishings to add style.

• New lamps of varying heights are strategically placed to serve different needs.

• Functional window treatments fashioned from burlap, grommets, and electrical conduit pipe keep the refined industrial style at the forefront.

• The room divider keeps storage racks and containers out of sight.

When the *Design on a Dime* team approached this room, the space already had a lot going for it: a vaulted ceiling, attractive exposed beams, and warm wood floors, not to mention a nicely finished antique desk. It made sense to work these elements into the final design. This is an important key to decorating on a budget: If you don't have enough time or money to start completely from scratch, you need to determine what's working and play it up. Here, paint, an interesting mix of materials, and a smart floor plan enhance the existing features of the space.

An Arrangement That Works

Along with the great mix of materials, the new arrangement pulls this space together. Originally, the room was a hodgepodge of filing cabinets and other storage pieces surrounding a cramped

(A) The cool purple wall perfectly frames the beautiful garden outside. (B) These once-cluttered bookshelves now display favorite photographs and books in an orderly fashion. (C) A movable divider wall conceals a large open storage area. The wall can be moved around the room to reconfigure the space.

work space and a makeshift meeting table. The space is now divided into three distinct sections: a work space with a desk, a storage area for shelves and cabinets, and a sitting/meeting area with comfortable furnishings. The smart layout allows plenty of space for each need, and no area feels cramped.

Upon entering the space visitors step into an inviting meeting area with a sofa, two chairs, and two tables spray-painted bronze, all arranged in a comfortable conversation grouping. The chairs are constructed of chrome and leather, materials that tie in with the overall look of the room; the openness of the chair design adds to the refined-meets-industrial look. Table lamps provide ample task lighting. A large sisal

Establish the Overall Look

Starting with a room that already had a cozy cottage feel, the homeowner incorporated a mix of "refined" (the antique desk) and "raw" (the office furnishings); this was the perfect starting point to give the room a jolt of style. The juxtaposition of refined elements and industrial materials—shiny corrugated metal, metal-accented furnishings and accessories, rough burlap and a textural sisal rug—is inviting and comfortable because the room is spacious and the new layout is flexible. The once dull and disorderly work space gains a fashionable new look.

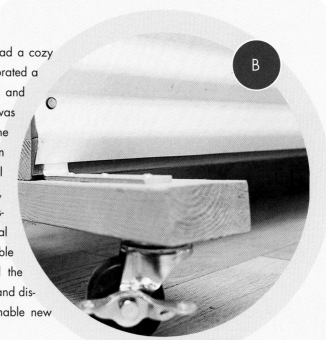

I love the idea of rough, raw, and textural. I've been drawn to burlap, but I've always shied away from using it ... now burlap will be the perfect solution for this office space. —Summer Baltzer on her window treatments

rug unifies the furnishings and complements the rough texture of the burlap window treatments. All the furnishings and accessories in this grouping were purchased at a used furniture outlet, which is a great place to visit when you need lots of items for little money.

Next to the meeting area stands an antique desk with a dark finish; the piece is within easy reach of bookcases and shelves. The desk is nicely framed by the soft purple wall behind. An existing pine table, spray-painted bronze, provides additional work space. Revitalizing this old table saves money and ties it to the industrial features of the room.

The back portion of the room is dedicated to storing work-related and recreational items, such as books, videotapes, and bicycles. Storage pieces were previously scattered throughout the room, cluttering the wide-open space. The new arrangement keeps all needed items within reach, and the sheet metal divider wall disguises the area with industrial flair.

Spruce Up the Space with Color

To bring a splash of color into the room, a grayed purple is chosen; it complements the wood tones of the floor and windowpanes, and it perfectly frames the lush green garden seen through large picture windows. To avoid overpowering the room—and to help establish the focal point windows and desk—the purple is applied only to two small walls, which face each other. To complement the dominant purple, a neutral beige is chosen for the burlap window treatment, the sofa, the two chairs, and the sisal rug.

Divide and Conquer

One of the best features of this room is its flexibility, provided in

Ⓐ The existing antique desk is right at home in the newly styled space when paired with a sleek new chair.
Ⓑ Wheels, strong enough to support the weight of the wall frame and metal, make the wall a versatile feature of the room.

part by a movable divider wall. This 6x10-foot wall, constructed of 2x4s, painted gray, and covered with corrugated sheet metal, makes the storage area disappear while creating an inviting space by framing the meeting area. Outfitted with wheels, the wall can be easily moved aside, allowing large items to be moved into and out of the space with ease.

Ⓐ The meeting area has stylish yet comfortable furnishings; the textural sisal rug and divider wall physically define the space. Ⓑ Charles evaluates many types of metals before selecting corrugated at a metal supply shop, which is often the most economical source of materials—and the selection is better than many home improvement centers.

Window Treatments Bring It Together

The combination of materials in this office space gives the room real design flair. The window treatments, hung from industrial conduit pipe, are a case in point: Inexpensive burlap—available in a range of colors beyond basic brown—isn't a typical choice for window treatments, yet its rough texture contrasts nicely with the gleaming metal finishes elsewhere in the room. The easy-to-create curtains can be opened to allow in light and views during the day and closed in the evening to conceal office equipment from the outside. Privacy—at any time of the day—is only a curtain pull away.

Table Facelift

Need a quick pick-me-up for a worn table? Think spray paint! Giving this old pine table a brand-new look was quick and easy—and very inexpensive—with dark bronze spray paint. For a similar look, first sand off the existing finish. Wipe with a tack cloth to remove any dust or particles. Apply one even coat of paint to the table, following the manufacturer's instructions; let dry. Lightly sand the surface again, wipe with a tack cloth, and apply another coat of paint.

BURLAP WINDOW TREATMENT

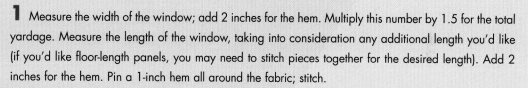

Choose burlap for a window treatment that adds textural punch. This inexpensive fabric—Summer purchased hers for $2.99 a yard—has a coarse weave that works in many decorating styles. It comes in many colors besides beige and makes a great alternative to the unattractive miniblinds that commonly grace office windows.

Although Summer created her panels with the help of a sewing machine, a large hand-sewing needle or even fusible hem tape will work equally well (test the chosen tape on a piece of scrap burlap to ensure a satisfactory bond).

C Industrial (metal grommets and chain, conduit pipe, shower curtain rings) meets textural (rough burlap) in this one-of-a-kind window treatment.

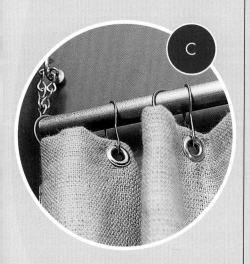

You Will Need

Burlap*

Tape measure

Sewing machine, matching thread, straight pins

Grommet kit, hammer

2 cup hooks, screwdriver, screws

Conduit pipe, cut to window width*

Thin-gauge chain, cut 6" longer than pipe*

Shower curtain rings or other hooks

Curtain pull

***Purchase these items after you've measured your window.**

1 Measure the width of the window; add 2 inches for the hem. Multiply this number by 1.5 for the total yardage. Measure the length of the window, taking into consideration any additional length you'd like (if you'd like floor-length panels, you may need to stitch pieces together for the desired length). Add 2 inches for the hem. Pin a 1-inch hem all around the fabric; stitch.

2 Using the grommet kit and hammer, insert a row of evenly spaced grommets along the top edge of the fabric, about 1 inch from the top (Photo A). Insert the shower curtain rings or other hooks into the grommets (Photo B).

3 Stitch the curtain pull to the upper left-hand corner of the window treatment. Attach the cup hooks to the wall, above the window frame. Thread the chain through the conduit pipe (Photo C). Thread the pipe through the shower curtain rings. Hang the chain from the cup hooks.

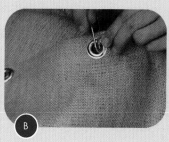

STYLE (101)

Week after week the *Design on a Dime* teams transform rooms that often have no definite style to speak of, creating spaces that look great and function well. Usually the teams get their inspiration from the homeowners' ideas, for instance, an existing piece of furniture or a specific mood or attitude they want to convey. If you are ready to redecorate a room but aren't

Ⓐ Slim-line metal-leg stools with molded black plastic seats and backs paired with bold artwork set a contemporary tone for this room. See page 18 for this room.

sure what type of look you are after, review the basic styles outlined here. As you will discover, it's often the furnishings that set the mood of a room, and all other decisions stem from them.

Many rooms are an amalgamation of styles; the dominance of one style over the others creates a look. And that's really what most people are seeking— the look of country or the look of traditional, for example, rather than a strictly enforced style. The easiest way to understand or discern a style is to look at various furniture pieces and look for clues. Here are four style examples and their identifying factors:

Contemporary

Sleek lines with minimal embellishment define contemporary styles. Contemporary materials such as plastic and industrial/commercial materials are used in home furnishings. Metal is a popular material: chromed steel tubing for the framework of a chair, for example,

and corrugated steel panels attached to the wall for texture and visual interest. Colors are frequently bold and clearly man-made as opposed to natural in tone. For example, the minimal furnishings and deep taupe walls, along with an emphasis on the strong angles of the counter, carry the style all the way through the room *left*. Review this room further (on pages 18 to 25), and you'll discover that even the overstuffed sofa, which has a traditional shape, suits the overall look of the room because of its bold color, contrast trim, and graphic pillows.

Traditional Country

Florals, plaids, stripes, lots of color, curvy lines, and comfy furniture define the traditional country look. A common incarnation of country is cottage, a look that uses all of the above in a pastel palette. An abundance of warm wood tones and flounces of fabric anchor country in its cozy zone. The bedroom shown on page 34 (and on pages 110 to 115) is firmly planted in a cottage look: pine furnishings, tall slender lamps with ornate columns and curved shades,

B Warm knotty pine furnishings set a country tone for this room. The clean lines and muted color note a modern flair. See page 136 for this room.

A A curvy pine headboard, a bundle of pillows, and lavender on the walls anchor this room in a traditional country cottage style. See page 110 for this room.

PAUL CEZANNE ~ Midday L'Estaque

A

lilac-color walls, and a contrasting green on the closet doors that give the appearance of a country armoire. White sets the closet apart from the wall, and the green accentuates the arched beaded-board insets of the doors.

Contemporary Country

When the busy look of country blends with the simpler look of modern, a room takes on a sophisticated but relaxed charm. A blend of these styles allows you to use furnishings that might look out of place if one style dominated the room. For example, a very modern lamp blends into the mix rather than stands out. Start with a limited palette; one clearly dominant hue will give the room visual cohesiveness. Consider the room on page 33 (and on pages 136 to 141). The warm knotty pine furnishings are classic country, but the clean lines and muted color of the sofa add a modern touch.

Ethnic Looks

International styles with Eastern influences add an exotic flair to rooms. Determine their origin and their compatibility for your decorating

C Bamboo, plants, and neutral tones temper the bold black and red scheme in this Asian-style room. Soft lighting adds to the serene feel. See page 62 for this room.

plans by looking at the same elements: line, color, and material. Asian and Moroccan styles (shown here), are good examples. Both styles have a spiritual sensibility, yet each takes a very different approach. One fun way is to watch movies set in the locale you're seeking to replicate. Set designers research many of the details to ensure the movie sets look authentic, so you can benefit from their hard work. Look for elements that strongly convey an exotic feel.

Asian styles often feature crisp, clean lines and natural tones. Bamboo is strongly associated with Asian styles, especially the Japanese style. The deeply relaxing, or Zen, feeling that Asian styles impart seems to come from the restrained nature of the style: Any ornamentation, such as the intricate carving on the stool *top right*, stands out in the simplicity of the room. The style is best interpreted by using a limited palette and incorporating natural materials, such as jute rugs, as this space does (as seen on pages 62 to 69).

Moroccan style uses more color and detail than Asian-style rooms do. If you desire an exotic space like this, review the room *left* (and shown on pages 80 to 85) to see the details, such as arches, dark wood tones, brass, and jewel-tone colors like blue, purple, and red, that will pull the look together.

B Moroccan arches, deep jewel tones, and metals with the look of distressed brass instantly convey the sultry land of Morocco. See page 80 for this room.

Furniture Styles Set the Tone

Unless your intent is to become an interior designer, a general understanding of furniture styles is all you need to decorate your home in any given style. Most American-based furnishings fall into one of two main categories, traditional and contemporary, that are fairly easy to distinguish. Cabriole legs on wing chairs, round-arm sofas, and inlaid-wood tabletops are some of the features you'll find on traditional American furniture. Colonial, Federal, and country styles are based on traditional furnishings. Curved tubular-steel chair legs, leather sofas, and glass-top tables are usually contemporary-style furnishings. Some contemporary furniture styles have the word modern tacked on: midcentury modern, Moderne, and Scandinavian modern, for example.

Much variation can be found with a particular style, and you're sure to find crossover between even the two key groups. In the past few years there's been a movement to incorporate sleek lines into country; the result is a hybrid called modern country or contemporary country.

A

BEFORE

GROWN- UP COTTAGE STYLE

A collection of hand-me-down furniture can make a room look cluttered and unstylish. However, if you look closely at your assortment, you may find similarities between dissimilar pieces (for instance their color or shape); then you can unify them further with the right wall color and accessories. Once the best pieces are saved and the rest are removed, a sensible arrangement will add functionality to the space.

Design Team

Sam Kivett, Summer Baltzer, Charles Burbridge

The Situation

• This living room is filled with odds and ends handed down from family and friends; the space lacks cohesiveness.

• The furnishings line the walls.

• The white walls are cracked and damaged.

• The natural focal point, a faux fireplace, isn't given the attention it deserves.

• The plentiful windows bring in light and views, but they are dressed in dull miniblinds.

The Solutions

• Some stylish furnishings—that suit a relaxed cottage style—are retained, but most are replaced.

• The furnishings are arranged to create a cozy conversation grouping.

• To make the most of the walls—without repairing them—a yellow fresco treatment is applied.

• A collection of empty frames is displayed on the mantel, along with a large mirror swagged with flowing fabric. A collection of white candles is stacked on risers in the firebox.

• The windows are now covered with sheer curtain panels hung from wrought-iron rods that complement the other iron accents in the room.

Arranged for Conversation

Creating a functional floor plan that could host a crowd or an individual (watching TV or reading) was a key goal in this room. Formerly, all the furnishings lined the perimeter of the room, creating a large open space in the center that wasn't very inviting; the arrangement didn't let the eye settle on one key element. With a better arrangement and additional furnishings that complement the old, the room is now a cozy, casual space that's a pleasure to be in.

First, the pine armoire with wrought-iron pulls, which houses a TV, is moved to a corner of the room. The TV can now be comfortably viewed from any area of the room, and the large armoire no longer overwhelms the fireplace—and its placement doesn't obstruct window views. This stylish piece—with its warm pine wood tone—is a hallmark of comfortable casual

Ⓐ The new arrangement allows for conversation and TV viewing. Ⓑ Simple touches like fresh flowers contribute to the casual feel in the newly decorated space. Ⓒ Because of its quality, comfort, and interesting mix of pattern—all important factors—the existing sofa is retained.

style, and it complements the overstuffed sofa and other cottage-style pieces in the room.

Using the best of the homeowner's furniture, including the large green sofa previously positioned against a long blank wall, a cozy conversation grouping is created around the fireplace. A coffee table and side chair fill out the grouping, and a vintage wing chair helps cement the eclectic style. A rug unites the furnishings and brings together the colors now present in the stylish space.

Enhancing a Ready-Made Focal Point

Establishing a focal point is an important consideration in any room, and it's a top priority in

mirror gives dimension and depth to the bare firebox. Small risers that fit into the box are topped with tall candles to mimic the look of a real functioning fireplace.

To complete the fireplace redo, a collection of inexpensive empty photo frames lines the mantel top. The frames, in various shapes, sizes, and styles from simple to ornate, create a pleasing grouping. A distressed window joins the group and rounds out the focal point display. A large mirror hangs behind the frames. Mirrors are a welcome addition in almost any room; they add depth with their reflective qualities and provide a place to primp before heading out the door. However, the large mirror above the mantel was more of a problem than an asset. To

In an effort to enliven these otherwise dull white walls and address the cracks, I'm applying this faux finish. It's a really simple and easy treatment that anybody can do. —Summer Baltzer

rooms where people gather. A focal point gives the eye a place to land and draws attention to important features. Initially this room lacked a clear focus: The furnishings lined the walls, creating a cluttered look; no one piece stood out from the rest. The faux fireplace was a natural focal point. However, it was surrounded by tall, overpowering furnishings, and the mantel showcased only a few small items that lacked impact.

To give the fireplace the attention it deserves, the cracked, discolored hearth tiles are treated to a dark maroon/black paint/glaze mixture. The mixture is brushed onto the tiles and grout, then mottled with a rag. The rich color grounds the fireplace and is a warm complement to the wood floors. A custom-cut

soften its appearance, a sheer scarf is draped over the mirror, masking the straight lines and nicely outlining the collection of frames.

Soften the Space with Fabric

Part of the charm of a cottage-style room is the combination of distressed finishes and breezy

---

Ⓐ A slim shelf hung on the wall offers stylish display space; the mirror above allows the homeowner to primp before heading out the door.

Ⓑ With the tall armoire moved to the corner, the fireplace now takes center stage.

Working with Hand-Me-Downs

In this room, leftover furnishings—from friends, family members, and former roommates—intermingle with new, more "grown-up" pieces. When redecorating keep what works and dispose of what doesn't. Someone else may be able to use what you edit out. Hang on to functional pieces that need only minor changes. For instance, add new hardware to an old dresser, paint or refinish old furnishings, or reupholster or slipcover an existing chair or sofa that's still comfortable. If you have surplus furniture you can't bear to part with, move it to another room or store it for later use.

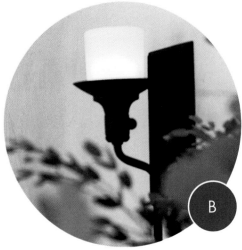

Display Shelf

A simple shelf positioned on a wall is a great place to stash items such as keys and display photographs and other keepsakes. In this room a shelf is set on custom-cut and distressed corbels that complement the overall cottage feel in the room. If creating corbels seems daunting, look for ready-made brackets at home improvement centers. Brackets are available in many shapes, styles, and sizes, and can easily be personalized with paint, stain, or other embellishments.

fabrics. In this room, sheer window treatments conceal the ordinary miniblinds, and swagged fabric softens the hard edges of the mirror on the mantel. The blinds serve a practical purpose while the treatments, hung from wrought-iron rods, add to the overall cottage-style look.

Use Liabilities as Assets

This room was previously a white box. To make matters worse, the walls were damaged and could have required costly, time-intensive repairs. The team decided to enhance the existing walls instead, using a summery Italian fresco paint treatment. Created with a mix of sunny yellow paint and glazing medium and applied to the walls with a rag, this treatment adds to the overall "shabby chic" feel in the room. Rich color settles into the cracks and crevices, giving the walls depth and dimension. The soft color is a perfect backdrop for the warm wood tones present in the room; it allows the dominant furnishing, the over-stuffed green sofa, to take center stage.

Ⓐ A collection of inexpensive frames from a secondhand store lends itself to cottage-style decor. Ⓑ Wall sconces, placed near the wall shelf, provide ambient light. Ⓒ The once-neglected fireplace is now a stunning focal point, thanks to a painted hearth, a mirror and candles placed in the firebox, and artfully arranged frames on the mantel.

Attention to Details

Decorative accents and small details are important to any room makeover, and this room is no exception. First, because the homeowner likes to display personal photographs, a custom wall shelf is created to fill the vacant space on the long entry wall. Set on carved and distressed corbels that capture the cottage feel, the shelf has plenty of space for photographs and other mementos. The mirror above it is a great place to primp before leaving the house. An extra corbel finds a home on the distressed sofa table as a stylish bookend.

Next, new lighting is added. The large windows bring in ample natural light; however, ambient and task lighting were missing. To rectify the problem, sconces are added to the long wall, and lamps are set on the sofa table, providing the right amount of light for reading.

Finally, the large rug, which unites the furniture grouping, pulls together all the colors present in the room, including the sunny yellow walls, the deep green sofa upholstery, and the rich maroon hearth tiles.

Ⓐ This sofa table with a distressed, worn appearance is the perfect complement to the relaxed cottage style chosen for this room.

FRESCO PAINT TREATMENT: COLORWASHING

In this room, a faux finish—with the look of an Italian fresco—enhances the overall "shabby chic" feel. The technique, colorwashing, is perfect for walls in need of repair: The glaze/paint mixture will settle into the cracks, producing a textural look.

Colorwashing works best if you begin with a light color, such as white or off-white. The light base color will allow the top glaze/paint mixture to have more visual depth. The technique is easy to master, allowing beginners to experiment with different tools, such as a brush, rag, or sea sponge; glaze/paint ratios; and application pressure to achieve various looks.

What Is Glaze?

Translucent glazing mediums, available at paint stores and home improvement centers, allow paint to stay wet and workable longer than it does when it's used alone. Glaze, which comes both tinted and untinted, adds depth and dimension to a surface. When working with glaze for the first time, mix different glaze-to-paint ratios until you get the look you want. The more glaze you add to the mixture, the more transparent the effect, which means more of the base coat color will show; for more coverage, add less glaze to the top coat paint.

You Will Need

Satin or semigloss latex paint for base coat in white or off-white

Satin or semigloss latex paint for top coat in desired color

Glaze

Paintbrush or roller, paint tray

Bucket, mixing tool

Application tool, such as a sea sponge, rag, or brush

1 Apply the base coat to the surface; let dry.

2 Mix the glaze and top coat paint in the desired ratio (2 parts glaze to 1 part paint is a good place to start) (Photo A). Water may be added for increased translucency.

3 If using a sea sponge or rag, apply the glaze/paint mixture to a 4-foot-square section of the wall, rubbing it over the area in a circular or figure eight motion (Photos B and C). If using a brush or other similar tool, apply the mixture to the wall in a crosshatching X motion. Note that with this technique, all brushstrokes will be seen if you are painting on a smooth wall; the more textured the wall, the less noticeable the brushstrokes will be.

4 After the 4-foot-square section is complete, immediately begin applying the glaze/paint mixture in an adjacent 4-foot-square section. Blend and smooth the areas between the sections while the glaze from the previous section is still wet and workable. Continue the process until the wall is complete.

A

B

C

FOCAL POINTS (101)

Whenever you enter a room, your eyes land on a key feature; that feature—the focal point—visually anchors the space. A room without a clear focal point seems unbalanced, and you feel a bit adrift as you enter. Often that happens when there's either too much furniture or almost nothing in the room. Architectural features and large pieces of furniture naturally

A bumblebee zips across a warm yellow wall. The inviting color and the fun figure raise the wall to focal point status. See page 92 for this room.

dominate a room, making them easily recognizable focal points. Fireplaces and entertainment armoires, for example, fit the bill in many living rooms. In a bedroom, the bed is generally the largest piece, so it's often the focal point, but often it needs to be played up with the addition of a headboard or inviting bedding and stacks of plump pillows to command attention. However, it's possible to promote a smaller piece to focal point status. For example, a large piece of artwork or a grouping of pieces hung strategically in the line of sight may visually override a dominant piece or feature in the room. Moving the seating pieces can also guide the eye to a different view.

The *Design on a Dime* hosts and designer coordinators sometimes play up existing focal points in the rooms they restyle; other times they create new focal points with new furnishings or decorative accessories such as artwork. If you are having difficulties creating a focal point in a room, consider these approaches:

Play Up a Fireplace

It's almost impossible to make a fireplace drop from dominance in a room, so the smart choice is to maximize its appeal. Create an interesting mantel display with groupings of items such as vases, candles, and framed photographs of different heights and sizes, and when the fireplace isn't in use or the fireplace isn't functional, put up a screen or an arrangement of white candles to make sure the firebox isn't a black hole.

Add Some Art

Often the first thing you see when you enter a room is a blank wall. Adding a new, interesting paint color to the wall as well as a framed print or a grouping of photographs will give the space more personality and draw people into the room. Or, put a single interesting piece of furniture against the wall, such as an armoire, a console table with a lamp, or a bookcase.

B

B When you enter this small room, your eye is drawn to the fireplace, but not over-whelmed by the size of it. See page 36 for this room.

Rely on the View

If your room has been blessed with a large window or a great view, show it off! Paint the trim a color that contrasts with the surrounding wall for extra punch. If there's no trim, add it: Home centers have a wealth of ready-to-paint or -stain moldings perfect for adding architectural detail to a window. Window treatments—from simple valances and gauzy tab-top panels to tailored Roman shades and even shutters—in eye-catching fabrics can bring attention to a window.

Use Space to Bring Focus

Design on a Dime's Kristan Cunningham says a focal point will gain more importance with breathing room. For example, if you have one item to showcase, it will have more significance if it has some visual space around it. But scale is another consideration. A small vase placed on a tabletop that stands against a large wall isn't a focal point—although there is wide-open space around it. If the space around the vase is reduced, for example flanking the tabletop with cabinets, the piece is brought into focus.

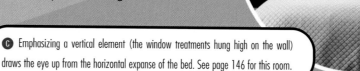

C Emphasizing a vertical element (the window treatments hung high on the wall) draws the eye up from the horizontal expanse of the bed. See page 146 for this room.

C

BEFORE

A BEDROOM FOR TWO

With all the toys, games, and clothes that clutter a child's bedroom, creating a fun, safe environment can be a challenge. When two children share a space, the problems are doubled, especially if the space is small. Repositioning the furnishings in a smart way to allow plenty of space for sleep and play, corralling the clutter, and providing small privacy zones transformed this space into an ideal haven for 6-year-old twin sisters.

Design Team

Sam Kivett, Summer Baltzer, Charles Burbridge

The Situation

• The bedroom has practical bunk beds. However, poor organization prevents the girls from living comfortably with the furnishings.

• The blue-painted walls are dull. The pastel-print window treatments lack excitement.

• Bins filled with toys, games, and art supplies are scattered throughout the room, making the room appear cluttered.

• There is insufficient lighting for all activities.

The Solutions

• New functional furnishings—bookcases, a worktable, and chairs—are combined with the existing pieces and organized to create different areas within the room for all the girls' activities.

• To bring fun and color into the lifeless space, the walls are treated to yellow and pink stripes, painted freehand. Hand-dyed window treatments complement the fresh color scheme.

• The bins previously lying around the room are now concealed in the closet.

• A lamp on the new dresser, a clip light on each bed, and a hanging ceiling fixture over the new work space address the lighting problems.

Arranged for Two

Children's rooms are more than a place to sleep; they are used for play, homework, and just hanging out. Therefore, the first thing to consider is the layout. How do you accommodate all these activities without crowding the room? Previously the furnishings in this room were pushed to the sides, and clutter overtook the space. To make the room more kid- and activity-friendly, it is divided into distinct areas that cater to different needs: sleep, play, and storage. The new "suite" gives each girl her own private space, so the twins can each perform individual tasks without getting in each other's way.

A Bed Is More Than a Place to Sleep

Comfortable beds are necessary in any bedroom, and they are especially important in kids' rooms, because kids use

Ⓐ With the addition of a canopy, the bunk beds are now a private oasis for the young residents. Ⓑ Egyptian figures cut from felt adorn the canopy. Ⓒ A large dresser easily accommodates the belongings of the two girls. Originally an unfinished piece, it was stained like the bunk beds.

them for relaxing and playing, as well as sleeping. First, clip lights are attached to each bed; they offer the perfect amount of light for late-night reading. Second, a breezy net canopy, the main attraction in the room, is added. The canopy features movable Egyptian-theme motifs made from felt and embellished with paint, glitter, and googly eyes. It offers a unique play space and provides a hideaway where the girls can get away from the outside world.

A A fresh coat of paint, colorful trinkets, and sparkly glitter bring this once-dark-stained mirror to life. B Clip lights attached to the beds provide task lighting for late-night reading.

The bunk beds were in terrific shape; the natural-finish wood was attractive, and the overall style and functionality made them worth keeping in the room. Bunk beds take up less floor space than twin beds and thus lend themselves to a shared space. By salvaging the old beds, the *Design on a Dime* team had enough money to address another need: a dresser.

The old dark-stained dresser was too small to accommodate the needs of two girls. At the foot of the bed, a new larger dresser now stands, creating a dressing space. The unfinished piece is the right size and scale for the room, and with two coats of clear varnish, it matches the natural

EASY EMBELLISHED MIRROR

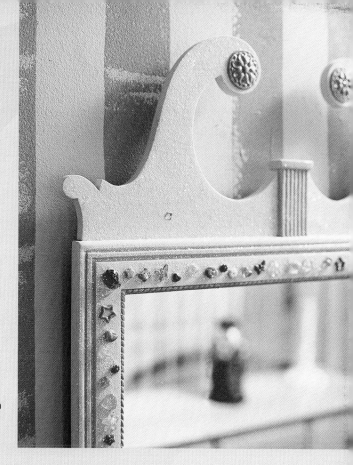

Giving new life to old, dated furnishings requires no more than a fresh coat of paint. In this room, the mirror, which functioned well, had a dark-stained finish that didn't fit the fresh, fun look the *Design on a Dime* team desired. To update the mirror and transform it into instant artwork, paint, glitter, and some playful accents are applied to the frame.

Not for Kids Only

This dressed-up mirror project can be translated into one suitable for an adult's room: Paint the mirror in a solid color (or colors) that complements your decor. You can either leave it as is or add buttons, seashells, mosaic tiles, small twigs, or other "grown-up" items to take the mirror to the top of the style chart. Regardless of whether it is just painted or you add trinkets, protect the mirror with two coats of polyurethane, omitting the glitter as desired in the steps *right*.

A great way to save money on any room redo is to revamp an existing piece of furniture.
—Charles Burbridge

For a video demonstration of this project and more *Design on a Dime* ideas, visit HGTV.com/dod

You Will Need

Mirror
Latex paint in desired color (base coat and optional accents) and finish, paintbrushes
Painter's tape, newsprint
Jewels, trinkets, or other small items
Clear-drying tacky glue
Water-base polyurethane, paintbrush
Glitter in desired color
Protective covering

1 Spread the protective covering on the work surface. Using painter's tape and newsprint, mask off the mirror portion.

2 Paint the mirror frame with the base coat paint; let dry. If needed, use additional coats for complete coverage, allowing the paint to dry between coats. If desired, use accent colors to highlight details on the mirror frame.

3 Using tacky glue, adhere the jewels, trinkets, or other small items to the mirror frame in any desired pattern (Photos A and B); let the glue dry.

4 Apply a coat of water-base polyurethane, following the manufacturer's instructions; let dry. Apply a second coat; immediately after application sprinkle the entire surface with glitter (Photo C).

5 Remove the tape and newsprint.

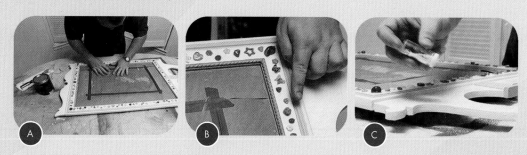

appearance of the bunk beds. It also costs much less than a finished piece would. This is the beauty of unfinished furnishings: They can be painted or stained to coordinate with nearly any piece you already have, saving you the expense of purchasing matching pieces—and the frustration of discovering that a set has been discontinued when you need to purchase another piece.

A Place to Play

All children enjoy various indoor activities, including art projects, playing with dolls, and racing toy cars. Providing adequate space to accommodate all these activities is essential. In this room the young residents didn't have much space for drawing and coloring. Now a large

that hangs over the desk provides lighting for evening hours.

Nearby, the bookcases stand at the ready with books, supplies, and cherished keepsakes. The items used most often are placed on the lower shelves, within easy reach of the children. These heavy freestanding furnishings are anchored to the wall to reduce the risk of the pieces falling onto the children.

Storage Savvy

Storage is an issue in any child's room; two children means double the clothing, toys, and books. Whatever the amount of storage space, parents

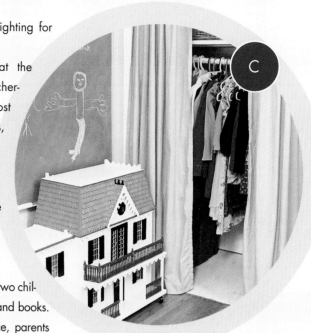

All children enjoy various indoor activities, including art projects, playing with dolls, and racing toy cars. Providing adequate space to accommodate all these activities is essential.

white desk with two chairs makes an ideal place to draw and do homework. The desk is placed in front of the window, so it receives natural light during the day. The new pendant light

must make the most of it. This room was previously filled with toys and clothes; it felt unorganized and crowded. To help keep the room clutter-free, the closet is reworked for maximum space. An upper shelf is removed so the shelf below can be stacked high with space-saving bins and pretty baskets, which previously took up valuable floor space. The labeled bins keep the room clutter-free and accessories, toys, art supplies, and other small items organized. The new large dresser stores additional clothes in a tidy fashion, freeing up closet space.

Ⓐ More than a place to sleep, this bedroom offers ample space to do homework or draw, thanks to a desk, two chairs, and a hanging light fixture. The bookcases keep art supplies and books within easy reach.
Ⓑ Charles touches up the stripes along the ceiling line.
Ⓒ The once unorganized closet is now orderly; a hand-dyed curtain conceals the storage space.

B

Color and Fun Accessories Are Key

To encourage creativity, children's bedrooms need to have a dash of color and fun. This room was short on style, with unattractive blue walls, mismatched furnishings, and toys scattered about. Now, bright, playful colors and accessories bring life into the space.

First, the walls are treated to an eye-popping pink and yellow-orange stripe treatment. The

Ⓐ A large roller cage with two small rollers and a spacer between is the tool of choice for creating freehand stripes. Ⓑ Charles searches for a dresser that's large enough to accommodate the clothing of two girls but not so large that it looks out of scale in the room.

loose, imperfect stripes are the perfect backdrop for the newly designed space; taped-off, crisply painted stripes would have been too grown-up and formal for the fun room. To coordinate with the new wall decor, inexpensive cotton curtains dress the windows; they're positioned over black-out shades that offer privacy and light blocking. Identical curtains cover the closet opening. Dyeing ready-made curtains is quick and easy and adds a balance of solid color to the room—a great money-saving technique. More bursts of pink appear in plump floor pillows. Special touches like the pillows make a room more inviting for young children.

A

Shared Spaces

Sharing a bedroom can teach valuable lessons, such as compromise and respect for others' possessions. Follow these cues to help make your children's shared space one they are proud to call their own:

• Sharing works best if children are close to each other in age and of the same sex because sleep schedules and privacy needs are different for children of varying ages and sexes.

• All children require a place to call their own, and when two share a room, it's even more important to carve out a niche for each one within that space. This can be as simple as dividing a portion of the room with a large movable chalkboard or converting a closet into a reading nook.

•Give each child enough space to store his or her possessions. Also, let the children express their individual personalities through displayed collections or prized items, such as stuffed animals, trophies, or framed photographs.

PLAYTIME CANOPY

A canopy can be more than a way to draw attention to a bed: It can provide a secret hideaway for a child and/or function as a play space. This large canopy is embellished with felt cut in Egyptian-theme motifs; the motifs are pinned to the canopy so they can be moved around. If your child prefers a different theme, such as cars, nature, or music, look for ready-made templates and stencils at an arts or crafts store.

C Using safety pins, Summer attaches the felt cutouts to the ready-made net canopy.

Taking my cue from the girls and their love of pyramids and horses, I'm creating an Egyptian-theme canopy from felt ... Every kid needs a canopy or fort.

—Summer Baltzer

You Will Need

Canopy

Felt squares in a variety of colors

Ready-made templates or stencils in the desired motifs*

Disappearing marking pen, scissors, fabric glue

Glitter paint, googly eyes, and other desired embellishments

Safety pins

4 plant hooks, screws, screwdriver

*If you can't find templates in the motifs you desire, make your own with cardboard or stencil plastic.

1 Using the disappearing marking pen, trace the motifs onto the felt. Cut out each shape and glue shapes together as desired (for example, the foliage and trunk of a tree); let dry.

2 Using fabric glue, adhere embellishments to the motifs, or use glitter paint to outline the motifs (Photos A and B); let dry.

3 Securely screw the plant hooks into the ceiling, above the four corners of the bed.

4 Hang the canopy from the plant hooks (Photo C).

5 Using safety pins, attach the motifs to the canopy in the desired locations.

A

B

C

A

BEFORE

INSPIRED BY AFRICA

Do you have a small room that tries to serve too many functions and doesn't perform any of them well because of awkward furniture arrangement and insufficient space? This room suffered from exactly that problem. It served as an office, guest bedroom, and storage space. With fresh furnishings and a new layout, this room illustrates how to create a practical yet inviting space that suits your most important needs and lifestyle.

Design Team

Lee Snijders, Summer Baltzer, Charles Burbridge

The Situation

- This tiny space currently serves as a guest room, office, and storage area. The little-used queen-size bed dominates the space, while one desk in a cramped corner struggles to accommodate two working people.
- With its bland pale-peach walls and minimal decorating, the room lacks excitement.
- The lighting is insufficient.

The Solutions

- To turn the room into a true home office with comfortable lounging spaces, the bed is removed. This allows space to create two workstations joined by bookcases for storage and display. A window seat is also added, which is perfect for curling up with a good book.
- For an exotic, global design theme, the *Design on a Dime* team introduces bold color with rich red paint and brings in artwork and trinkets from the homeowners' frequent travels—along with rattan furnishings and a breezy mosquito netting canopy.
- Hanging fixtures over the window seat and desks provide ample ambient and task lighting.

Working at home has many advantages, but an ill-conceived office design might leave you searching for space in which to perform necessary tasks. Such was the case in this room: The combination guest room/storage area also functioned as an office, with little space for actual work areas. Because both homeowners need to use the room for various activities, the layout—dominated by a little-used queen-size bed—wasn't working. Rethinking the furnishings, playing up the best features of the room, and incorporating some exotic decor created a room that is ideal for work and play. If you are faced with a similar situation, take heart: A little planning and a dash of creativity will get you the results you want.

Work Space Is a Priority

First things first: What is the main function of the room? In

Ⓐ This office has the right furnishings for work and relaxation, including desks and a comfy chair. **Ⓑ** The room is filled with texture, from the nubby pillow fabric to the woven rattan chair. **Ⓒ** This custom window seat is a simple box with open cubbies for displaying treasures below. Summer's upholstered cushion makes this a comfy place to sit and relax.

this case, some tough choices had to be made. Because the homeowners required work space more than a guest room, the bed was removed to make way for ample work areas. The room also performs another important function: storage. Closed storage—a spiffed-up vintage trunk—hides unsightly clutter, while open shelves show off collectibles and keep books and other office essentials within reach.

To prevent the homeowners from bumping elbows, desks are set up on opposite sides of the room, with the large picture window as a focal point. Matching bookcases flank the window. These bookcases both support one end of each desk and provide storage and display space. To take advantage of the natural light and views, a custom window seat fills the space between the two bookcases. This cozy nook, complete with a comfy cushion and soft plump pillows, offers a place to kick off shoes, relax, and read or nap in the warmth of the sun.

A A vintage trunk with a distressed paint finish continues the travel theme. **B** A canopy makes the chair become a private hideaway, while a custom bulletin board provides ample space to tack up notes. **C** The desks are now part of larger wall units that provide easy access to books and essential office supplies. Now two people can work at the same time—without bumping elbows.

Lighting Solutions

Lighting is a major consideration for every room, from kitchens to home offices, and each room has specific needs to address. Most rooms require a blend of general, task, and accent lighting, with each strategy concentrating on a different need. General or ambient lights give a uniform, overall glow that comes from one or more sources. Task lights are positioned to provide light where you need it for specific jobs, such as above a work area. Light fixtures—inverted baskets—are positioned above each desk in this room, and inverted and decoupaged wastepaper baskets provide the right amount of light for reading and writing at the window seat. Accent lights focus light on an object or surface, such as artwork or an architectural feature, for the purpose of highlighting it.

Red provides a bold background for the decorative touches that now fill the room, including the decoupaged trunk and bulletin board.

Room to Relax and Enjoy

Determining a new configuration for the work-stations is only one part of the task; ensuring that the homeowners want to spend time in this room is another. Because the homeowners have an impressive collection of travel-related accessories and artifacts, a Moroccan theme with an eclectic mix of world travel memorabilia is selected. To bring the theme to life, the once pale-peach walls are covered with a rich red paint, which complements the dark-stained wood, rattan furnishings, and the hardwood-look linoleum floor. The red provides a bold background for the decorative touches that now fill the room, including the decoupaged trunk, bulletin board, and framed prints.

The light fixtures above the window seat are plastic wastepaper baskets embellished with colorful scraps of tissue paper. Woven baskets outfitted with pendent light fixtures provide task lighting above the desks and rattan chair. The large rattan chair is draped with mosquito netting and topped with a cushion and pillows. The chair offers another place to rest and relax.

Ⓐ Decoupage is a great technique for personalizing accessories such as bulletin boards. Ⓑ This room gets plenty of daylight, but lighting was a problem at night. Light fixtures hung over the window seat, the desks, and the rattan chair are the solution.

DECOUPAGED LIGHT FIXTURE

Jazz up an ordinary plastic wastepaper basket with tissue paper; turn it upside down and attach a pendant light fixture, and you have a one-of-a-kind light source that costs a lot less than equivalent fixtures at the store.

Lightweight tissue paper in eye-popping colors is cut into shapes that complement the exotic flair in this home office—stylized diamonds, scallops, and circles. For your fixture cut shapes that suit your individual space and style. For more-precise motifs, use templates or stencils available at arts and crafts stores.

These homeowners have a laundry list of lighting needs in their new space ... A plastic wastepaper basket of all things proved to be my solution.
—*Charles Burbridge*

You Will Need

Plastic wastepaper basket
Tissue paper in the desired colors
Scissors
Decoupage medium, small paintbrush
Crafts knife
Pendant light fixture kit

1 Cut the desired motifs from the tissue paper. Turn the wastepaper basket on its side and position some of the motifs on the basket to determine the most pleasing arrangement. Continue cutting motifs until you have enough pieces to complete the design.

2 Working one small section at a time, apply decoupage medium to the outside of the basket. Using the small paintbrush, position the tissue paper motifs on the basket, applying additional medium as needed to ensure that the edges of the motifs lie flat (Photo A). Continue applying the motifs to the basket until the design is complete; let dry. Cover the entire basket with a thin even coat of decoupage medium to seal; let dry.

3 Using the crafts knife, cut a hole in the bottom of the basket, making it large enough to accommodate the light fixture (Photo B).

4 Insert the light fixture into the hole and follow the manufacturer's directions for hanging (Photo C).

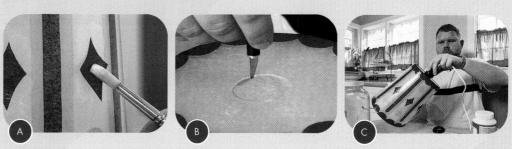

RECOLOR YOUR ROOMS

BLAND (TO) BOLD ON A BUDGET

The living room is often the first room people see upon entering a home. It needs to set a welcoming tone for visitors, yet still function as a private place to relax and entertain. This space lacked style; however, thanks to the *Design on a Dime* team, it is now steeped in functionality, bold color, and Asian flair, providing a warm greeting for all who enter.

Design Team

Sam Kivett, Summer Baltzer, Charles Burbridge

The Situation

• Seating space for entertaining is limited: One sofa must serve all seating needs.

• The space lacks sufficient lighting. One window brings daylight to the space and overhead lighting, accent lighting, and other fixtures are absent.

• The white walls are a stark contrast to the black sofa and the green carpeting.

• The open floor plan doesn't allow for separation between the living room and kitchen.

The Solutions

• The comfortable sofa stays, but additional seating—ornately carved side tables that can serve as ottomans when topped with comfy pillows—is added to provide enough space for guests.

• The window still plays a central role in the lighting pool. A shade is added for privacy and light control. A bamboo fixture is hung from the ceiling and stylish lamps handle task lighting.

• To complement the Asian decorating scheme, a combination of tan and red is used on the walls.

• Rearranging the furniture and introducing a room divider creates visual separation between the living room and kitchen.

Authentic Color

To bring an Asian theme to life in this space, the first area to address was the white walls. Earth tones, such as browns, reds, and black, are common colors in Asian decor. A rich suede-tan color was chosen for two walls, and a bold red was used for the focal-point wall, the first wall seen upon entering the space from the outside. For good coverage, two coats of each color are used; although applying two coats is more time-consuming than one, it provides the most even coverage and reduces the chance of white patches peeking through.

Black accents make their way into the room in the existing sofa; red, brown, gold, and cream appear throughout the room in the artwork, pillows, and decorative pieces. Furnishings in deep wood tones complement the earthy colors in the room and round out the Asian theme.

A New colors and textures give the living area a warm, intimate atmosphere. The sofa faces the windows, and the armoire houses the TV. B Sushi bar accessories accentuate the Asian theme. C A custom bamboo/paper lantern fixture provides general illumination.

A Smart Arrangement

One of the goals of this makeover was to visually separate the living room from the kitchen, a difficult task in a small space. The solution is multifaceted: The first step was to move the sofa away from the focal-point wall. The large piece seemed out of proportion in the small space; pushed against the long wall, it called too much attention to itself. Now the sofa faces the window, providing a natural division between the two spaces and letting artwork on the focal-point wall take center stage.

To enhance the division between the rooms, a custom bamboo divider stands directly behind the sofa. The bamboo poles are placed at angles to mimic the natural tendency of the plant. The divider is light and airy and doesn't overpower the room the way a solid divider might.

ornate details hold luxurious gold and black silk pillows. The pillows can be moved to the sofa or floor for added comfort wherever guests relax.

To round out the arrangement, a low coffee table is added in front of the sofa. Purchased at an import store for less than $200, the dark wood table has clean lines and flared legs reminiscent of an Asian pagoda. If additional table space is needed, the pillows can easily be removed from the side tables.

Light Up the Space

Living rooms require a combination of light sources to accommodate quiet conversation,

Import stores really have an eclectic range of furniture, and they're exotic and cheap. This table has the great Asian lines we were looking for ... this is perfect. —Summer Baltzer while shopping for furnishings for this room

Previously, audiovisual equipment sat on a small table across from the sofa. The clutter of equipment is now housed in a red-painted cabinet that's positioned beneath the window. The size of the cabinet doesn't interfere with light or views. When the doors are closed, the TV and stereo components are concealed, and the decorative hardware and patina of the piece add visual interest to the space. On top, artwork and foliage find a home.

Because this room is used for entertaining, seating was an issue. The sofa doesn't allow flexible seating arrangements for group conversation or TV viewing. Low side tables offer a solution: The dark-stained tables with

---

Ⓐ Low ottomans can function in two ways: When topped with pillows they provide extra seating; take off the pillows, and they serve as additional table space.

Quick and Easy Area Rug

The green carpet in this living room didn't fit the clean-lined Asian look the *Design on a Dime* team wanted to create. Because the carpet in this apartment can't be removed, a large floor covering is needed to mask the unappealing color—at little expense. The solution? Four large rush mats, purchased for only $10 each, are connected with double-sided carpet tape to create one large area rug. The floor covering unifies the area, and its texture blends well with the overall look, giving the room a comfortable organic feel.

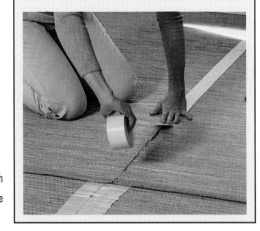

BAMBOO ROOM DIVIDER

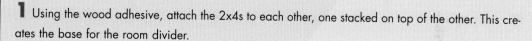

Nothing says Asian decor better than bamboo. This versatile material is used for multiple decorative purposes—including table runners and light fixtures, as shown in this room—and here it is fashioned into a one-of-a-kind divider that visually separates two areas. The airy appearance of the divider balances the dark colors and weight of the other furnishings. When searching for bamboo for this or any project, keep the end use in mind. For this project slender pieces are chosen for a natural, organic feel, which thick, beefy pieces could not provide. Shop import or cane/basket supply stores for the best variety of bamboo at the best prices (pieces for this project were purchased for $1 each).

We wanted to do something that not only balanced and separated the living room from the kitchen space but also left an open feel and didn't close the room off entirely.
—Charles Burbridge

You Will Need
7' lengths of bamboo (approximately 30 pieces)
2x4s (2)*
Strong wood adhesive
Dark wood stain, paintbrush, rag
Drill with paddle bits

*Purchase the 2x4s in lengths to suit your individual needs; in this project the boards are the same length as the sofa.

1 Using the wood adhesive, attach the 2x4s to each other, one stacked on top of the other. This creates the base for the room divider.

2 Following the manufacturer's instructions, stain the 2x4 unit.

3 Select a paddle bit that matches the diameter of the first piece of bamboo (Photo A). Drill a hole into the top of the 2x4 base, letting the bit enter at a slight angle. Apply wood glue to the end of the bamboo piece and insert the bamboo into the hole (Photos B and C).

4 Repeat Step 3 until a pleasing arrangement has been created. Randomly space the bamboo along the top of the base, inserting it at various angles for a natural, organic feel.

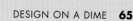

B

reading, and entertaining. This room had no light source except one large window. Completely uncovered, the window brought in natural light in the day, at the expense of privacy. A rice paper shade now dresses the window; it is lightweight enough to let in light when closed and offers privacy at night. The airy look of the shade blends with the other elements in the room.

To address the need for overhead light, a fixture is created. Varying lengths of bamboo are crisscrossed to form a grid that supports suspended paper lanterns. Attached to the ceiling above the coffee table with plant hooks, the grid is wired with strung wire and light sockets, eliminating the need to wire the fixture through the ceiling, a potentially costly endeavor.

A floor lamp is added near the sofa for task lighting. The black metal base and white paper shade with a black bamboo motif perfectly complement the space.

C

Ⓐ Positioning the sofa with its back to the kitchen creates a defined living room space. Ⓑ Asian touches are evident throughout the space, from a bamboo-print lampshade to inexpensive artwork. Ⓒ Summer finds a dark wood table that perfectly complements the Asian decor for less than $200.

Temper a Dominant Element

Previously, the living room color scheme was overwhelmed by green carpeting. To lighten the carpet, the homeowner originally chose a beige rug, but it was too small to successfully do the job. Because the green doesn't complement the new Asian decor, more-complete coverage is needed. Four highly textured rush mats butted against one another and joined with double-sided carpet tape fit the bill, and they cost less than a single large rug would. The new floor covering suits the Asian theme and, along with the bamboo divider, helps visually separate the living room from the kitchen.

Accessories Bring It All Together

The stark white walls were once unadorned; the homeowner propped a few pictures against the walls, but none found a home at eye level. Now the freshly painted red and beige walls are at home with artwork featuring Asian characters and scenery, a fitting addition to the space. To further accentuate the theme, a tea set, Asian-style pottery, a bamboo table runner, and foliage with angular lines are introduced.

A Twine is used to tie the bamboo poles together for the overhead light fixture. **B** The divider is constructed from airy bamboo poles, randomly positioned to resemble how bamboo plants grow in nature.

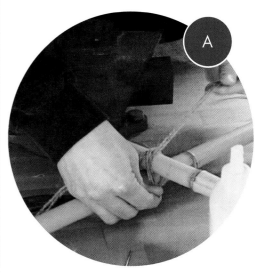

Custom Overhead Lighting

This room had no overhead lighting—or any light source other than a large picture window. For a one-of-a-kind solution to this lighting shortage, readily available materials are brought together: bamboo poles, twine, glue, electrical wiring and light sockets, and Asian-style paper lanterns. First, the bamboo poles are arranged in a grid pattern in a shape and dimension that suits the area above the sofa and coffee table. Then the poles are connected with twine and dabs of glue for a strong bond (Photo A). Once the grid is complete, electrical wiring is strung along the poles; instead of being connected through the ceiling (not an option for renters), the wire will run along the ceiling and down a wall, where it will be connected to a socket. Next, the wired grid is hung from plant hooks on the ceiling, and light sockets are attached to the wire (Photo B). Paper lanterns of different sizes are hung from the fixtures at varying heights, creating visual interest (Photo C).

COLOR AND PAINT (101)

Paint color generally pops up as the first question when a room redo begins, and it's often the first thing people comment on when a room is done. The color in a room, especially the color on the wall, has great impact. The rooms the _Design on a Dime_ teams tackle are often void of wall color, making paint a top priority. Is choosing a paint color causing you

(A)

(A) Spencer prepares to roll paint onto a wall. The striking gold color will require two coats for complete coverage; white patches may show through if one coat is used.

dismay? _Design on a Dime's_ Charles Burbridge has five tips to help guide you:

1. Trust your instincts! Everyone's perception of color is unique. A yellow that is cheery to some is sure to be nauseating to others. Choose a color that you like. Who cares what the next-door neighbors think? Ignore the tried-and-true tenets of color theory. If you have always wanted a lime green bedroom with magenta trim, then I say "Go for it!".

2. Your existing color scheme is an important consideration when you're selecting a new paint color. Check to see if the new color you've chosen works with the furniture you already have (unless you're intending to purchase new furniture). New accent pillows can be added to a sofa to help tie it in with the new color; however, a large-scale reupholstery job can be costly. Also, keep in mind that colors you've used in adjoining rooms

might be visible from the freshly painted room; choose the new color accordingly for a harmonious overall look.

3. Start with a quart of your dream color and paint a few test areas. Choose test areas in different parts of the room to get the full effect. If the color doesn't look right, at least you're only out the cost of a quart, not the cost of two or three gallons.

4. Color changes with changes in light, so look at your test areas throughout the day and in all the lighting conditions available in that room. The difference can be drastic, so be scientific about this review process; keep notes. A deep wine color might be lovely and warm during the day. However, at night, in low light, it can appear black.

5. Remember: It's only paint! Maybe lime green and magenta wasn't the best color combo after all. Relax. No paint treatment is permanent; you can always paint over it.

How to Paint a Room

Prepping a room before painting is nearly as

important as choosing the colors.

For general room painting, you'll need the following items:

• An angle-bristle brush. Choose a high-quality synthetic-bristle brush.

• A roller and at least two roller covers with the correct nap thickness. Choose a roller that has a comfortable grip, a cage that spins easily, and an antislip device at the end to keep the roller cover from edging off. Also, look for inexpensive disposable paint tray liners (these eliminate the task of washing the tray).

• Drop cloths to cover the floor all the way to the edge. Use drop cloths to cover any furniture that remains in the room. Canvas or paper/poly drop cloths are non-slip and durable.

• Plenty of painter's tape to ensure crisp lines. This is especially important when painting around molding and window frames.

Once you have gathered the necessary supplies, prepare the room for painting. Skipping this step can cause problems later: Removing paint splatters from furnishings can be difficult if not impossible! Take the time to do each of the following tasks:

• Wash the walls and let them dry completely. For most rooms, a standard household cleaner will remove dirt and grime.

• Remove as much furniture as possible, and use drop cloths to cover built-ins and large pieces that are too heavy to move.

• Remove switchplates from electrical outlets and light switches, or tape around them.

• Tape off all molding around doors, windows, ceilings, and floors.

• Patch and sand all holes in the walls.

Now you are ready to paint!

• Whether your room has fresh drywall or several layers of old paint, primer provides the base you need for a high-quality finish.

B This kitchen has a bold mix of colors: Bright green doors are set against crisp white cabinets, and the walls are painted a sunny gold. See page 154 for this room.

• Using the angle-bristle brush, paint around outlets and light fixtures and cut in around floor and ceiling molding.

• Dip the roller in paint. Start by painting a large W in the middle of the wall, then glide the roller up and down to smooth out the paint. The motion of painting the W shape evenly distributes the paint from the roller on the wall, so when you smooth it out with long floor-to-ceiling strokes, you'll get an even coat.

C Spencer and Kristan look on while Dave pours a rich golden color into a paint tray. To eliminate splatters on the floor, the carpet is covered with a heavy drop cloth.

A

BEFORE

NICE  NEUTRAL

Sometimes you have all the right furnishings to suit your needs in a particular space, as well as accessories to pull the look together—yet something still doesn't seem quite right. The culprit may be color. This dining area had everything going for it—great furnishings, beautiful hardwood floors, and good-quality artwork—but it lacked cohesion. Now it's filled with new colors and accessories that complement, not overpower, the groundwork for a striking room.

Design Team

Kristan Cunningham, Spencer Anderson, Dave Sheinkopf

The Situation

• The room has stark white walls, with hardly any artwork adorning them.

• One oddly placed light on the ceiling illuminates the space.

• The space is filled with warm wood tones, but no additional color is present to balance them.

• The dining set is functional and in good condition. Its proportions suit the space, but it doesn't feel grounded.

The Solutions

• One wall is painted a deep gray color; two ledges that can serve as planters or display space bring attention to the newly painted wall. On another wall the existing prints are arranged to take better advantage of the space.

• The original ceiling fixture is removed, and three custom light fixtures are hung directly above the table.

• New chair coverings warm and soften the space.

• A banded sisal rug—in a dark gray that complements the gray wall—grounds the dining set.

Calming Color

When the question of color comes up, people often think of bright bold hues that can enliven their rooms. However, calmer, subtler choices can be equally effective. Neutrals, such as browns, grays, and whites, can bring life to a space without being boring. In this room, charcoal gray is chosen to emphasize one wall (the other two walls are connected to a sunken living room; leaving these walls white helps them to blend with the rest of the open space). This dark charcoal color contrasts nicely with the warm wood tones present throughout the room, and it brings focus to the long wall. Previously, the white crown molding and white door were lost against the white wall, but now they "pop" against the gray.

Two plant boxes are attached to the wall to enhance its focal point status. The fresh green grass in the boxes adds a soft natural element to the clean-lined space. If

---

A The existing dining table still looks great in the space, but moved away from the wall it allows for improved traffic flow. **B** and **C** A tailored striped fabric in navy and red dresses up the dining chairs. Some chairs are treated to new drop-in seats; others gain classy slipcovers.

A

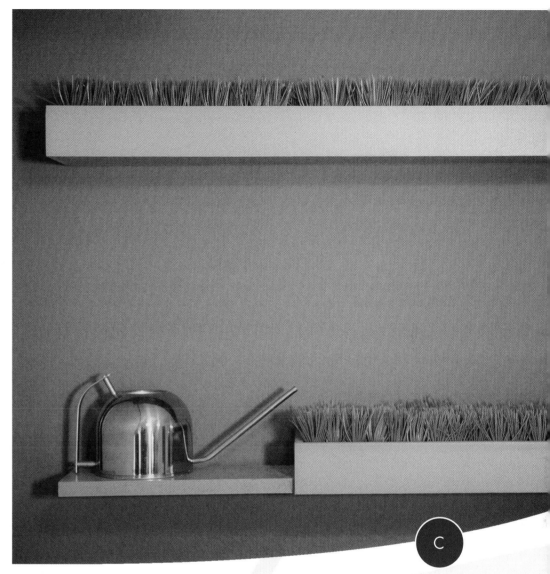

Textural Table Runner

Sometimes it's the simplest touches that pack the most punch! In this clean-lined dining room, details bring interest to the space. The long pine dining table would look too bland if nothing adorned its top. Three inexpensive circular rattan place mats form a sleek centerpiece, a creative alternative to a frilly tablecloth. Stained and then connected with leather lace, the place mats are treated to a coat of polyurethane for protection because the space is washed frequently.

the homeowner tires of the grass, the boxes can be topped with acrylic plastic and used as shelves. Another dose of cool natural color comes from the artichokes displayed on the table.

Enliven with Fabric

Extra doses of color enter the room through fabric on the chairs. Six of the dining chairs are treated to new drop-in seats. The crisp navy pinstriped fabric fits the overall look of the room and serves as another rich color contrast to the wood tones. The other two chairs—those that stand at each end of the table—are given a

more tailored treatment: cream-color slipcovers with navy pinstriped fabric skirts, cinched with a leather strap. The leather is another natural touch that accentuates the contemporary space.

Illuminate the Entire Space

This dining area lacked sufficient lighting, a common problem in many homes, old and new

---

Ⓐ The deep gray focal-point wall serves as an interesting contrast to the white paint and light wood tones present in the space. Ⓑ A mirror hung at one end of the dining room makes the space seem larger. Ⓒ Slim planters with springy green grass introduce a splash of color and texture.

alike. One brushed-nickel overhead fixture, hung at one end of the room, provided what light it could. The table had to be positioned beneath the fixture, close to the wall for adequate lighting. For better general illumination and to eliminate the "hot spot" created by the original single pendent fixture, three fixtures are hung on the ceiling. The paper and metal fixtures are an interesting mix of refined and industrial, and their straight lines complement other clean-lined elements in the room, such as the chair backs, pinstriped fabric, and black picture frames.

Deck the Walls

To keep a clean, uncluttered look in this dining room, the walls are minimally decorated. The

expanse of space in a creative way. The new focal-point wall was previously unadorned, except for a small clock that was barely visible because it was tucked into a corner.

On an adjacent wall, four framed prints previously hung in a tight gridlike grouping. The prints—small pieces of artwork surrounded by large white mats and understated black frames that draw attention to the colorful artwork—fit well with the new look of the room. However, the arrangement was too compact to have any impact on the large wall. For due attention, they are now arranged in a linear fashion, directly above a new sideboard. A mirror framed in brushed nick-

Bringing color into a space isn't limited to a warm or cool palette only: Neutrals, such as browns, grays, and whites, can bring life to a space without being boring.

wall-mounted planters positioned on the focal-point wall provide visual interest and a practical display space, as well as break up the large

About Color

The color wheel is divided into cool colors (between yellow-green and violet) and warm colors (between yellow and red-violet). In general, cool colors impart a calm feel, whereas warm colors make a room seem lively. The most successful color schemes often include a mix of cool and warm colors: Cool colors sometimes require a warm-up from the "active" colors, while warm colors can use a splash of calm to cool them down. Neutrals—white, black, grays, browns, and beiges—are sometimes considered to have no color, but they can have a great effect on warm and cool colors. When paired with neutrals, warm and cool colors have more dimension through lightness, brightness, darkness, and dullness because they take center stage.

el adorns the wall opposite the prints, giving the illusion of more space—a great trick to use in any small space that needs a visual boost in size, such as entryways and hallways.

An Arrangement That Works

The odd position of the table was necessary for decent lighting. However, the table was pushed against one wall, preventing people from maneuvering easily around the space. The room isn't wide enough to accommodate the table turned in the other direction, so the piece is moved away from the wall instead. In that position, it is evenly illuminated by the trio of new light fixtures. With the table pulled out from the wall, all diners—even those

---

Ⓐ Placed above a dark-stained sideboard, the existing prints command attention with a new linear arrangement.

Ⓑ This sideboard offers a stylish spot to display attractive glassware and provides storage for little-used dishware within.

on the ends—can move around comfortably.

A void was created when the table moved away from the wall. To fill the space—and to provide some much-needed storage—an ornate antique sideboard is added to the room. The piece can hold serving pieces inside, and the top can be used for displaying prized glassware or as a serving space in a buffet setting. The dark-stained piece contrasts nicely with the light wood tones present elsewhere in the space, giving a well-rounded feel to the room. Beside the sideboard stand two additional chairs, ready to be pulled into the seating pool when needed.

To ground the furniture arrangement, a dark sisal rug with a black band is placed beneath the table. The rug gives visual relief from the expanse of light maple flooring and unifies the dining set; the black band complements the gray wall, the picture frames, and the metal frames of the light fixtures.

Ⓐ The trio of new overhead light fixtures provides even illumination over the dining table and eliminates the bright "hot spot" created by a single fixture.

DROP-IN SEATS

With all its colors, motifs, and textures, fabric can have powerful impact in any space, including dining areas. For example, the addition of a tablecloth and new drop-in dining chair seats in a coordinating fabric can introduce color and pattern. Re-covering old, worn drop-in seats is a quick way to freshen dining chairs because the task requires few tools and materials.

Choosing Fabric

When planning to re-cover an old drop-in seat, select a stable fabric with a tight weave that can stand up to stretching. Look for one that is lightweight enough not to add bulk to the seat and make it difficult to fit into the frame. To test before buying, pull the fabric diagonally, vertically, and horizontally; the fabric should only "give" a little, and the threads should not pull apart, creating a hole. Another consideration: When selecting fabric, keep the scale, size, and style of the chair in mind. For example, an oversize floral pattern may overpower a small chair, while a tiny print may not balance the overall look of a large chair. Finally, consider who will be using the chair and whether the seat may require cleaning (for example, if young children will use it). Some fabrics are already treated with stain-resistant finishes, and spray-on finishes are often available at fabric stores and furniture stores.

You Will Need

Fabric in desired color and motif
Optional: High-density upholstery foam and polyester batting in desired loft, in size to fit seat; spray adhesive
Screwdriver, flat and phillips
Staple gun and staples
Pins
Scissors

1 Remove the seat from the chair, using a screwdriver if necessary.

2 Using the flat screwdriver, remove the staples that hold the fabric to the seat. Remove them carefully; you will use the old fabric as a pattern.

3 Lay the new fabric flat, right side down. Place the old fabric on the new fabric; pin in place and cut out.

4 If the old foam and batting are flat and stained, replace them with new high-density foam and polyester batting. Using the spray adhesive, attach the foam to the wood seat; top with the batting.

5 Center the foam- and batting-covered seat on the new fabric, right side down. Starting on one side, pull the fabric to the underside of the wood seat and staple at the center of the fabric edge. Repeat on the remaining sides, pulling the fabric taut. Continue stapling around the fabric until it is secured (Photo A). At the corners, neatly fold and staple. After stapling is complete, trim any excess fabric.

6 Replace the seat in the chair.

A

BEFORE

DINING IN A JEWEL BOX

Mismatched furnishings, assorted pillows, and ill-fitting table coverings can make a peculiar dining experience. A lack of color and a dated light fixture can compound the problems. With the help of Moroccan colors and design motifs, this dining room is magically transformed from so-so to sultry for less than $1,000. Take cues from this makeover if you want to infuse your dining room—or any other room of the house—with an exotic atmosphere.

Design Team

Sam Kivett, Summer Baltzer, Charles Burbridge

The Situation

• This dining room is filled with leftover furnishings, none of which suit the purpose of the room (the homeowner sits on the floor to dine).

• The room is completely void of color, with white walls and white carpeting.

• A balcony overlooking the living room makes the dining room feel spacious; however, sometimes a more intimate dining experience is desired.

• The sliding glass doors let in plenty of light; however, window treatments—and privacy—are missing.

The Solutions

• A new table and chairs get diners off the floor, and a buffet is added for entertaining and storage purposes.

• To set the room apart from the rest of the house, it is bathed in jewel tones.

• A movable divider screen, in a repeated arch shape typical of Moroccan design, can close off the room by concealing the balcony.

• Gauzy window treatments let in light, yet contribute to an intimate setting.

Jewel Tones Capture the Mood

This dining room is in a home that is decorated entirely in white—white walls and white carpeting. To set it apart from the other rooms—and to bring a touch of the exotic into the space—a Moroccan theme, rich with jewel tones, is chosen. These colors (blues, reds, and purples) impart an exotic feel; in this room, the bright, compelling hues are balanced with a neutral beige, present on appliqué panels attached to the walls and a folding screen.

The panels, which are nailed to the wall, are created from ⅛-inch wood paneling cut in a classic Moroccan arch motif. First the panels are painted with sandy beige paint; then, umber paint is applied to the surface with a stiff-bristle brush to give the panels dimension. A mixture of umber paint and polyurethane is then ragged onto the panels for even more

Ⓐ Moroccan touches abound in this space, from the jewel tones and arch motifs to the dark wood tones.
Ⓑ The finials on the curtain rods are large green glass balls wrapped in brushed-silver metal. Ⓒ Bright dishware and exotic-looking brass goblets and pitchers bring life to the table setting.

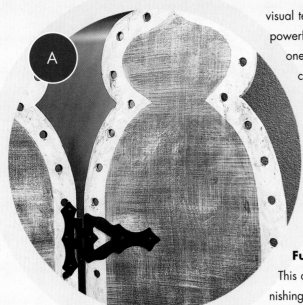

visual texture. This project is easy and packs a powerful design punch; a similar look (albeit one-dimensional) can be created with stencils and inexpensive acrylic paint.

The arches are the highlight of the Moroccan theme in this dining room. Repeated along the tops of the walls and on the screen panels, the arches unify the space. One arch would look out of place; a grouping gives the motif purpose.

Furnishings Suit the Theme

This dining room was previously filled with furnishings left over from other rooms of the home.

and backs; additional chairs may be added to the table for cozier dining.

To fill the space along one blank wall, a buffet is added. It provides serving space (eliminating trips to the kitchen), storage for wine and glasses, and a surface on which to display Moroccan-motif accessories. The dark wood and highly textured rattan door inserts fit nicely with the dining set.

Flexibility Is Key

Although this dining room had its problems—including lack of color and an odd groping of furnishings—it also had one strong point: implied spaciousness. A balcony with a waist-high railing

After Charles discovers that the beige paint on the arch appliqué motifs "needed a little something more," he flecks umber paint onto the motifs with a stiff-bristle brush, followed by a coat of water-base polyurethane.

A coffee table surrounded by pillows and covered with an oversize lace tablecloth was used as a makeshift dining table. A video cabinet filled with various trinkets and knickknacks was angled into a corner near the sliding glass doors. On-the-floor dining may work in an Asian restaurant, but it isn't terribly practical at home, especially when serving guests. Getting up and down to fetch items from the kitchen can become tiring—and guests can become uncomfortable from sitting on the floor.

To get diners off the floor, a round table is purchased for $60 at a thrift store. The table suits the space perfectly: It is in scale with the room, the dark wood complements the jewel tones and Moroccan theme, and the strong pedestal base gives the table center stage presence. The table is surrounded by four new chairs with dark wood frames and rattan seats

overlooks the main living area, creating an open feel. However, sometimes a more intimate setting is desired, especially when entertaining a small group. To make the space feel cozier, a versatile, movable screen is created, using motifs and materials that match the wall appliqués; the screen is hinged together with ornate black hardware. When it stands in front of the balcony, it closes off the space, enhancing the "jewel box" feel of the room. When it's not in use, the screen

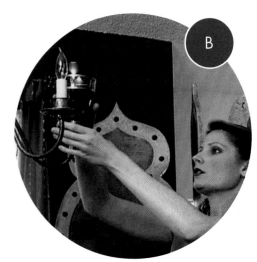

Ⓐ A custom room divider in a repeated arch motif creates an intimate setting when placed in front of the balcony. Ⓑ Summer puts the final touches on her customized chandelier.

EMBELLISHED CHANDELIER

Do you want a new chandelier? Are you short on money? Dress up your existing fixture with glass and metal paints, available at crafts and paint stores; the total cost will be significantly less than the price of a brand-new fixture. Choose colors that suit the style of your room and consider drawing freehand designs, such as dots and swirls, to make your chandelier truly one-of-a-kind.

You Will Need

Brass chandelier

Glass paint, red and gold (or other desired colors)

Metal paint, umber (or other desired color)

Painter's tape, in the desired width

2 small artist's paintbrushes

Clean rag

Paper plates

🄲 Summer dabs metal paint onto the chandelier; it was too old-fashioned to complement the room's new Moroccan-style look.

This dusty, sultry look is now perfect for the Moroccan theme.
—Summer Baltzer on her painted chandelier

1 Remove the glass globes from the fixture. Using painter's tape, mask off an area of each glass globe in the desired location, where you want the glass to remain clear. Note: In this example, the tape is placed about 1 inch below the top of each globe.

2 Pour some of the glass paint onto a paper plate. Using a small artist's paintbrush, paint the exposed portion of each globe red (Photo A); let dry. Carefully remove the painter's tape (Photo B). Using another small brush, paint narrow golden bands between the clear and red portions of each globe (Photo C); let dry.

3 Using a clean rag, dab the metal paint onto the brass portion of the fixture; let dry. Replace the globes in the fixture.

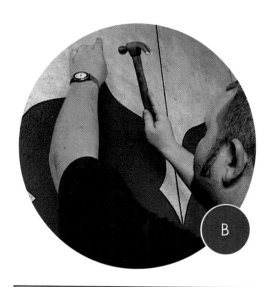

B

Revitalize a Wood Surface

Whether you find a table at a thrift store, similar to Summer's $60 find for this dining room, or you already have a table at home that needs a little care, help is as near as your local hardware store. Boiled linseed oil helps restore and enhance the finish of any wood furnishing, including tables and doors. Using a clean rag, apply the oil to the wood surface in circular motions. Allow it to sit for a few minutes; then remove excess oil with another clean rag. To maintain any wood furnishing, apply linseed oil to the surface once or twice a year.

C

can be moved elsewhere in the room, or it can be folded and stored.

Fantastic Fixture

This dining room has large sliding glass doors, which let in lots of natural light. However, at night the only light came from a colonial-style fixture that was too traditional to suit the new exotic decor. Because so much of the allotted $1,000 budget was used to furnish the room, the *Design on a Dime* team had to devise a plan to reuse the existing fixture. Help came in the form of inexpensive glass paint, applied to the globes, and umber-color metal paint, applied to the base and arms of the fixture. The resulting dusty patina perfectly fits the Moroccan theme.

Pulling It All Together

To pull the new look together, flowing fabrics, brass accents (including thrift store candleholders and a vase), and colorful ceramic dishes are introduced. The sliding glass doors were previously unadorned; to make them a more suitable focal point and to create a sense of privacy, sheer tab-top panels adorn the doors. Hung from a rod with scepters at each end, the treatments complement the design theme.

Ⓐ To bring dimension and additional Moroccan flair to the space, arch-motif panels grace the walls. Ⓑ Charles nails the wall panels in place with short brad nails. Ⓒ A small buffet offers a great place to stash dishware. Tall brass candlesticks grace its top and brass plaques adorn the wall above.

A

BEFORE

SOUTH-OF-THE-BORDER STYLE

The kitchen is a natural gathering space in the house: It's the place to cook, eat, and converse with family and friends. However, if a kitchen is filled with mismatched items, void of personality and style, and lacks sufficient light for the various activities that take place there, no one, including the cook, will want to spend time in it. In this kitchen bold color and fabrics create a space that's a joy to be in, and lighting and furniture arrangement satisfy the practical requirements.

Design Team

Sam Kivett, Summer Baltzer, Charles Burbridge

The Situation

• The white walls are bland.

• The long room lacks sufficient lighting for cooking and dining. Two mismatched, poorly situated ceiling fixtures illuminate the room.

• The pass-through between the dining area and the living space is unadorned.

• The rectangular table, in a light wood tone, is too large for the space.

The Solutions

• To add some zip to the room, the walls are painted yellow. Colorful new fabrics and decorative accents help bring the space to life.

• A custom grid of track lights is added above the kitchen work area. The globes of the ceiling fan are updated to boost its style.

• Custom artwork—faux stained glass—is hung in the pass-through to add interest to the space.

• A new round dining table with coordinating chairs fits the space better, and its wood tone blends with the others present in the room.

• Tab-top panels are customized with a lively striped fabric to cover all the windows in the room.

Start with a Sunny Color

This long galley-style kitchen and dining area was a mishmash of styles—country furnishings and a Victorian-style ceiling fan—surrounded by uninspired white walls. To bring a sense of uniformity to the space, a new decorating theme (Mexican), highlighted by a new color scheme, is chosen. For the walls an eye-popping yellow is selected. The warm hue brings energy to the space and brightens the dark, rich wood tones of the cabinets and other woodwork. The high-energy yellow is a vivid backdrop for other new colors in the space, including red (another warm color) and a cool green.

Furniture That Fits

The existing dining set didn't suit the space: The table was pushed against one wall to aid traffic flow. For groups larger than four, the table had to be pulled out, leaving little space

Ⓐ The new round dining table suits the space better than the old rectangular table. Ⓑ Wrought-iron touches abound in this kitchen, adding to the Mexican flavor. Ⓒ Updated globes on the existing ceiling fan give the fixtures a more contemporary look.

for anyone to move around it and making the French doors inaccessible. Adding to the problem was the light-tone finish of the pieces, which contrasted too much with the dark tones present throughout the space.

To make better use of the designated dining space in this kitchen, a 48-inch-round pedestal table and coordinating chairs, all with a rich dark finish, were purchased. At $450, this set consumed a large portion of the *Design on a Dime* team's $1,000 budget. However, when pieces are used so frequently—on a daily basis—it makes sense to invest in quality. The classic Mission-style pieces chosen for this room will stand up

cleanup area, a 1x2 grid system, painted white to blend with the ceiling, is suspended with white eye hooks and chain. The grid is equipped with a converter and six track lights, which can be positioned to illuminate any area in the kitchen. The converter allows the track system to be plugged into the existing outlets, eliminating the need for costly in-ceiling wiring.

Second, the ceiling fan fixture is updated with new globes. Originally, the fixture had scallop-edge globes, which were too stuffy-looking for the space. The new schoolhouse-style globes complement the hefty pedestal table and give the fixture a brand-new look for little expense. Because of their shape and style, the globes disperse more light.

When redecorating a kitchen, look to food for inspiration, choosing bold or muted shades of red, yellow, and green. Red heightens our senses of smell and taste, encouraging our appetites. —Lee Snijders

over time and adapt to nearly any decorating style. The new table is positioned directly below the ceiling fan, allowing plenty of space for movement around the table.

Bright Ideas

Insufficient lighting can spoil an otherwise pleasant room, and this is especially true in kitchens. A good blend of general, ambient, and task lighting is needed for every chore that takes place in a kitchen, from chopping vegetables to doing dishes. In this kitchen, the light wasn't centered over the work space, so darkness hovered over the range. A formal-style ceiling fan fixture lit the dining area. However, it didn't disperse enough light to evenly illuminate the room.

First, to shed more light on the cooking and

Ⓐ Colorful ceramic plates hung on the wall add bold color to the room.
Ⓑ The yellow walls are a sunny backdrop for the dark wood tones and green window treatments.

Dress the Windows

Kitchens usually have many sharp angular lines, from cabinetry to boxy appliances. Window

---

Table Talk

Choosing a dining table that fits your space and needs is an important consideration. The next time you need to purchase a dining table, keep the following pointers in mind:

• Standard table height is 30 inches. When selecting chairs to accompany your chosen table, allow 12 inches between chair seats and the tabletop.

• If space is limited, choose a round table. A small round table, about 4 feet in diameter, will comfortably seat four. If less space is available, look to multipurpose islands for casual dining.

• If you can't find the exact finish you desire, use paint or stain to get the look you want.

• If you purchase a used table, refresh the surface with linseed oil, as described on page 85.

Kitchens usually have many sharp angular lines, from cabinetry to boxy appliances. Window treatments can help break up the straight lines while letting in light or providing privacy.

treatments can help break up the straight lines while letting in light or providing privacy. In this space, the tall French doors were left bare, and the high windows above the table and sink had louvered shades that only covered the bottom portion of the windows. To dress up the windows, and to provide another punch of color in the room, a vivid striped fabric is stitched to the bottom portion of inexpensive extra-wide ready-made tab-top panels. These panels have been cut and hemmed to fit the dimensions of each

Ⓐ Accessories in primary colors "pop" against the cheery yellow walls.

Ⓑ To effectively light the cooking area of this kitchen, custom track lighting is created; the fixtures can be swivelled to illuminate different areas of the room.

window, eliminating the expense of purchasing double the number of treatments.

The green panels, accented with vivid stripes of red, yellow, and blue, offer cool contrast to the sunny walls. The striped fabric features some of the colors in the pass-through artwork. Other decorative touches, including plates hung on the wall and the bowl of fruit on the dining table, repeat key colors. These colorful accessories are decorated in motifs that enhance the Mexican scheme—and the accents are a great touch with little effort or expense.

To bring more attention to the windows, the treatments hang on black metal rods with decorative wrought-iron finials. Hung high on the walls near the ceiling, the long window treat-

ments nearly touch the floor, a design trick to visually heighten the space.

Perfect Pass-Through

The pass-through between the dining area and living room called for some sort of treatment that would give it more interest. A custom grid of framed faux stained glass fit the bill. Connected with chain and hung in the opening, the frames are stained to mimic the dark color of the cabinets and other woodwork; the warm yellow and red of the painted glass coordinate with the other hues in the space. The space between the frames allows a partial view of what's happening on the other side and maintains the open feel of the kitchen.

FAUX STAINED-GLASS GRID

Do you have a pass-through that could use a boost of style? This combination of inexpensive photo frames, glass paint, and hardware creates visual excitement and brings colors into an otherwise empty space. This piece is perfect for a pass-through, as shown; it can also make a colorful treatment for a small window, similar to a sun catcher.

C Before the addition of the faux stained-glass grid this pass-through was a blank space just waiting to be jazzed up.

BEFORE

The stained-glass technique is a great way to add color and visual interest anywhere you need it.
—Charles Burbridge

For a video demonstration of this project and more *Design on a Dime* ideas, visit HGTV.com/dod

You Will Need

Uniform-size photo frames, 16, or enough to fill your space
Pliers
Glass paint, red and yellow (or other desired colors)
2 paintbrushes
Stain, paintbrush, rag
Fine golden chain, screw eyes
Wire snips, drill with small bit
Plastic, newspaper, or other protective work covering
Paper plates
Tacky glue

1 Remove the glass and cardboard from the frames and use pliers to remove the metal tabs (Photo A). Set aside. Following the manufacturer's instructions, stain each frame completely; let dry (Photo B).

2 Pour some of the glass paint onto a paper plate. Paint half of the glass pieces red and paint the other half yellow; let dry.

3 Predrill two evenly spaced holes on each side of each frame (for a total of eight holes). Screw the screw eyes into each hole. Apply tacky glue to the inside edge of the frames; insert the glass pieces.

4 Lay the frames on your work surface in the desired pattern. Connect the frames with short (approximately 3-inch-long) pieces of chain (Photo C). Predrill eight holes into the top of the pass-through. Screw the screw eyes into each hole and connect the unit to the pass-through with chain.

BEFORE

NURTURING THE NURSERY

Making room for a nursery might seem like a difficult task when space is at a premium. In this home a weight bench occupied the chosen space. Moving the bench to another area was the first step in making this a soothing room. Still, the dull white walls made the room look clinical, not comfortable. To make the space suitable for a young prince or princess, the *Design on a Dime* team used timeless color and lasting motifs.

Design Team

Kristan Cunningham, Spencer Anderson,
Dave Sheinkopf

The Situation

- The room functions as a nursery and weight room.
- The white walls are boring and not engaging enough for a young child. No other colors are present in the room.
- The parents desire a theme that will grow with the child.
- Lighting is insufficient, the vertical blinds have a sterile look, and the bare hardwood floors need warming.

The Solutions

- The weight set is moved elsewhere in the house so the room can be dedicated to the baby.
- To spruce up the space, the walls are painted a pretty yellow, and a host of pretty colors accentuate the main hue.
- Nature—bugs, butterflies, and grass—is the chosen theme. This will suit a girl or a boy and will endure as the child gets older.
- The recessed fixture is replaced with a custom cloud unit made of acrylic plastic. Floor and table lamps are added for task lighting.

Color for Either Gender

This large room functioned well as a weight room, but its pristine white walls were far too sterile to be a comfortable nursery. Rather than traditional blue or pink, a sunny yellow is chosen for the walls. The cheerful color will suit a girl or a boy and is the perfect backdrop for a rainbow of hues used as accents for the space.

Fun Fabrics Dress It Up

Children's rooms are a great place to play with color and pattern, and this nursery is no exception. At first, this dull room was void of any personality: Unappealing vertical blinds covered the windows, and the white wall of closet doors, although eliminating the need for freestanding storage pieces, was uninspired. To make matters worse, the closet doors often became stuck on the track and were difficult to open.

A The chair and ottoman provide comfort for mom and dad; the nearby table keeps nursery essentials within reach. **B** The custom light fixture adds an ethereal touch to the space. **C** A soft-sculpture leaf and ladybug hangs near the crib, an interesting alternative to a mobile.

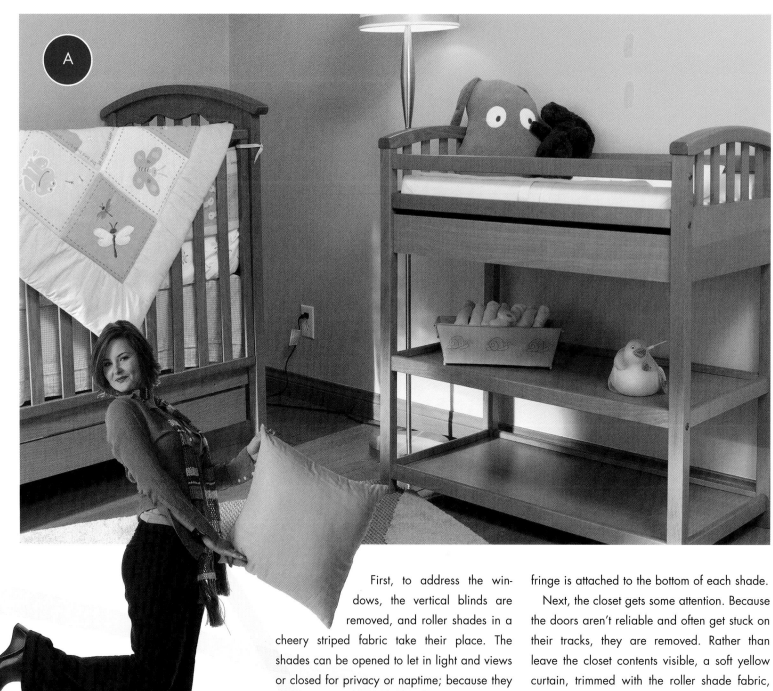

First, to address the windows, the vertical blinds are removed, and roller shades in a cheery striped fabric take their place. The shades can be opened to let in light and views or closed for privacy or naptime; because they are room-darkening, no light will enter during daytime naps. For a fun kick, colorful pom-pom

fringe is attached to the bottom of each shade.

Next, the closet gets some attention. Because the doors aren't reliable and often get stuck on their tracks, they are removed. Rather than leave the closet contents visible, a soft yellow curtain, trimmed with the roller shade fabric, covers the opening. Hung from an inexpensive, ordinary tension rod, the curtain can be easily opened, closed, and removed for laundering.

Custom Touches Catch the Eye

This nature-theme nursery is all about fun, and numerous special elements contribute to the mood. On the hardwood floor, a layered cov-

A The crib and changing table are positioned in one corner, opposite the windows. Both pieces have a warm honey wood tone that is accentuated by the sunny yellow walls. **B** A large floor covering, created from a sisal rug and green carpet remnants, adds color and texture to the hardwood floors. It also unifies the furnishings in the room.

LEAFY RUG

A mix of textured sisal and plush green carpeting combine to create a floor covering that's one-of-a-kind. This rug is fashioned to suit a bug-theme room; use your imagination to design a rug that suits the scheme in your room, for instance, a football field or checkerboard.

The great thing about customizing a rug is that you're not limited to the standard sizes, shapes, and patterns that you normally find in a store. I pulled this one in for less than $150.
—Spencer Anderson

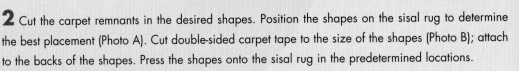

You Will Need

Sisal rug, in the desired dimensions
Carpet remnants, in the desired color
Carpet pad
Sharp utility knife
Double-sided carpet tape

1 Determine your design. In this example, the green carpeting cut in wavy shapes mimics lush green grass along a walking path (the brown sisal).

2 Cut the carpet remnants in the desired shapes. Position the shapes on the sisal rug to determine the best placement (Photo A). Cut double-sided carpet tape to the size of the shapes (Photo B); attach to the backs of the shapes. Press the shapes onto the sisal rug in the predetermined locations.

3 Using long pieces of carpet tape, attach the carpet pad to the back of the sisal rug (Photo C).

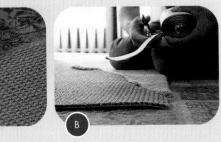

For a video demonstration of this project and more *Design on a Dime* ideas, visit HGTV.com/dod

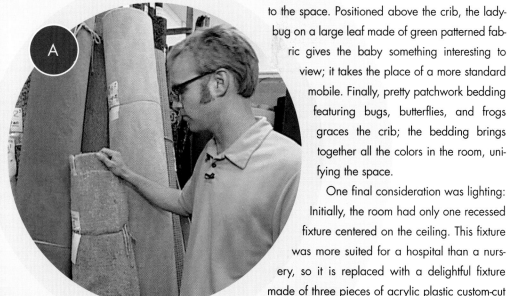

to the space. Positioned above the crib, the lady-bug on a large leaf made of green patterned fabric gives the baby something interesting to view; it takes the place of a more standard mobile. Finally, pretty patchwork bedding featuring bugs, butterflies, and frogs graces the crib; the bedding brings together all the colors in the room, unifying the space.

One final consideration was lighting: Initially, the room had only one recessed fixture centered on the ceiling. This fixture was more suited for a hospital than a nursery, so it is replaced with a delightful fixture made of three pieces of acrylic plastic custom-cut

The cheerful yellow will suit either a girl or a boy and is the perfect backdrop for a rainbow of hues used as accents throughout the space.

ering, created with a sisal rug and green carpeting remnants, warms the space. Resembling a garden path, the rug can be used as a play space as the child grows. With all the furnishings positioned around the perimeter of the room, the rug artfully fills the large void in the middle of the floor.

Bug images appear on the walls and bedding. On the walls, one buzzy bee is hand-painted in pretty pastel hues; the cheery insect leaves a looping path across the walls and closet doors. Hand-painting was easy enough in this case—the bee is created with ordinary geometric shapes, such as circles and ovals. For the faint-of-heart, stencils are available at arts and crafts stores and can offer the look of hand painting. Also adorning the walls is a soft sculptured piece of art that brings dimension

to mimic clouds. Two lamps join the lighting pool as task lighting, one beside the changing table and one on the nightstand. To dress up the ordinary white shades, grosgrain ribbons in different colors and widths are attached.

Double-Duty Space

Previously, this room served as both a weight room and a nursery. Claiming the space for the baby was as easy as removing the bench.

Ⓐ Spencer shops for carpet remnants for a custom floor covering; the selection is impressive. A plush green carpet best suits the leafy motif he plans for the rug. Ⓑ Dave uses a jigsaw to cut the acrylic plastic used for the cloud light fixture. The long blade allows him to cut quickly and easily through the thick material.

Designing a Smart Nursery

A nursery needs to be comfortable and functional as well as safe. Keep these suggestions in mind when creating a space for your little one:

Choose the right colors. Yellows, along with reds and greens, are gender-neutral colors that are more versatile than pink and blue. They lend themselves to many decorating schemes, so you can keep the wall color the same if you change the decor as your child grows.

Choose classic motifs. Novelty motifs may be cute now, but you'll end up replacing them in a year or two. Before you paint a large wall mural of a storybook character, consider other ways to bring it into the room—for instance, through inexpensive bedding or lampshades that can easily be replaced as your child grows.

Select the best crib. Ensure the crib you have chosen meets current U.S. Consumer Product Safety Commission standards. (If you are unsure, check that the slats are no more than 2⅜ inches apart; also check that there are no cutouts in the head- or footboard and that drop-side latches can't be easily released.) Also, look to the future when choosing a crib: A crib that converts into a toddler's daybed will eliminate the need to purchase another piece of furniture and will make the transition easier for the child. When positioning a crib in a room, place it away from window treatments with cords and away from heating and cooling vents. Placing the crib in the middle of the room makes it—and the baby—a focal point.

Choose versatile furnishings. Select furnishings that can stay in the room as the child grows. For instance, a changing table may later be used for a storage unit or makeup center.

Consider your own needs. As any parent knows, there will be nights when your baby is fussy, so incorporate furnishings, such as a daybed or recliner, that allow you to be comfortable when baby isn't.

Choosing a suitable arrangement for the furnishings—a crib, changing table, nightstand, and chair with ottoman—that allows smooth traffic flow and flexibility was the next task.

No furnishings are placed in front of the closet wall for easy access to the shelves and drawers. Across from the closet area stands the crib; as the only piece that lines the wall, it's an

instant focal point, enhanced by the soft sculpture above. The changing table stands along the adjoining wall, within easy reach from the crib. Rounding out the space is a chair and ottoman with blue fabric cushions, and a nightstand covered with a fitted white cloth.

The only addition is a daybed that stands between the nightstand and long closet wall. This bed serves many purposes: Mom or dad can rest there on nights when the baby isn't comfortable, and it can stay in the room as the child grows, to be used as a bed or as a getaway for reading and relaxing. It can also host guests in a pinch.

Ⓐ The long wall of closets is dressed up with cheery curtains hung on a tension rod. The curtains conceal the contents with more style than ordinary sliding doors. Ⓑ Spencer and Dave hang the new acrylic light fixture. Replacing an old utilitarian light, the cloud fixture perfectly suits the nature theme chosen for the room.

Stenciling 101

One easy yet exciting way to add color and motifs to a room is by stenciling. Ready-made stencils are widely available in arts and crafts stores in nearly any size and motif imaginable. If you've never stenciled before, here are some basic guidelines:

• After you determine where you want to place the motifs, apply stencil adhesive to the back of the stencil and position on the wall. The adhesive will prevent paint from seeping beneath.

• Use small bottles of inexpensive acrylic paints for stenciling; the range of colors is astounding! Pour a little paint onto a paper plate and dip a slightly dampened stenciling brush into the paint. Pounce the brush on the plate to eliminate excess paint; then pounce the brush on the stencil openings. Use a different brush for each color.

• When you are done, move the stencil to the next area and repeat the process.

HEAVENLY LIGHT FIXTURE

To bring the feel of the sky into this nursery, a custom cloud light fixture—created from three pieces of cut acrylic plastic—is mounted to the ceiling. For other rooms in the home, the acrylic plastic can be cut into about any shape imaginable.

G The one ceiling fixture in this room was more clinical—and suited for a hospital—than a baby's nursery.

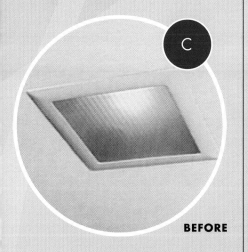

BEFORE

You Will Need

Medium-density fiberboard (MDF), permanent marker
Acrylic plastic sheets, spacers
Safety goggles
Jigsaw, router, orbital sander
Acrylic glue
Globe light fixture

1 Draw the desired pattern on the MDF (Photo A); cut out with the jigsaw. Trace the pattern onto the acrylic plastic three times (Photo B); cut out each piece with the jigsaw. Use a router to smooth the acrylic plastic edges and sand each piece to give the acrylic plastic a frosted look (Photo C).

2 Layer the three acrylic plastic pieces in the desired design, leaving the middle portion one layer thick (to be attached to the globe). Use the acrylic plastic spacers and acrylic glue to layer the pieces.

3 Attach the globe to the ceiling; thread on the acrylic plastic unit and secure with the cap.

A

BEFORE

WARMING A BEDROOM  COLOR

When your heritage directs you to purchase furnishings and accessories in colors and shapes with which you are familiar, in this case Asian designs, sometimes it's difficult to break the mold and combine them with pieces of different eras and styles that express who you are. In this bedroom, color, shape, and accessories unite disparate furnishings into one harmonious group. If you are in a similar situation, use the ideas shown in this makeover to bring balance to your space.

Design Team

Kristan Cunningham, Spencer Anderson, Dave Sheinkopf

The Situation

• The bland space, with white walls, white closet doors, and light-color flooring, needs a color pick-me-up.

• This large room is home to a mix of clean-lined contemporary and traditional Chinese furnishings, as well as mismatched accessories.

• The large windows provide natural light; however, the dark wood blinds are dated. Mismatched lamps contribute to a cluttered look in this room.

The Solutions

• A mellow green is chosen for the walls; a golden yellow dresses up the closet doors. Red accents on a custom bench seat add warmth and life to the color scheme.

• Color and shape are used to unify the existing furnishings. New accessories that complement the eclectic style are added.

• The windows are covered with bamboo shades and cornice boxes. A pair of custom lamps—with bases created from firewood and painted bright red—joins the lighting pool.

Yellow + Green = Comfort

Stark contrast—in color and tone—was one of the factors that kept this room from feeling pulled together. Initially, this wide-open space had white walls, an uninspiring row of white closet doors, beige carpeting, and dark-tone wood ceiling beams. The beams complemented the furnishings, but all the wood tones were in stark contrast with the boxy white room.

To pull everything together, a scheme of mellow green, gold tones, and jolts of red is selected. Green is typically considered a cool, calming color. However, yellow-green is warm and invigorating. The yellow-green in this space is a warm, almost neutral backdrop that makes the dark-tone furnishings look comfortable at center stage.

With the walls painted, the closet doors stood out more; however, they were bland in comparison to the walls. To pro-

A A punch of red stands out against the warm yellow-green walls. **B** The bamboo shades are in sync with the Asian decor in this bedroom. **C** Small touches, such as this dark-color clock, help blend all the styles in this room.

vide visual impact for little time and expense, tall rectangles are masked off with painter's tape and painted with a sunny gold tone. The vertical shapes, outlined by the original white, mimic the strong lines on the furnishings.

To turn up the heat in this room, red is chosen as a strong accent color. It appears in the upholstery that covers the new custom bench, on the matching pair of bedside lamps, and even on the existing small dresser.

Furnishings That Work

The homeowners had a blend of traditional Chinese furnishings (a chair and small dresser) and clean-lined contemporary pieces (a bedroom set). However, against a backdrop of white walls, the different furnishings fought with each other for dominance. By moving some key pieces, playing up the best attributes of each, and choosing new complementary accessories, all the furnishings live in peaceful coexistence.

The bed and matching nightstands were already in good position in the room (the bed couldn't move closer to the closets, and the size and shape of the room wouldn't allow placement beneath the windows). To bring the bedding up to par, first the frilly scallop-edge quilt and satiny pillows are replaced with striking gold and white striped bedding. Then, to make better use of the space at the foot of the bed, a tufted fabric bench is added to give the homeowners a place to rest and comfortably change footwear—and it provides a luxurious touch. The focal point is completed with the addition of a sisal rug beneath bed and bench; the natural textural

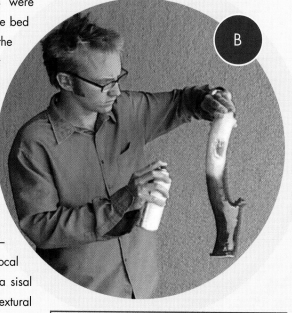

Ⓐ Luxurious fabrics, a large headboard with gridlike details, and striking artwork above make the bed a commanding focal point. Ⓑ Spencer paints the firewood bases of his lamps a glossy red. Ⓒ This once-bare corner is now home to a stylish freestanding mirror.

Custom Lamps

To bring a dose of color and organic form to this room, Spencer Anderson created a pair of lamps from firewood and two lamp wiring kits. Available at hardware stores and home improvement centers, lamp kits typically include a threaded rod, washers, and a harp holder. Specialty and decorative finials and bases are often available at lamp shops, and inexpensive shades can be found at any superstore. Nearly anything—a teapot or an urn, for example—can become a lamp. Pick up a lamp kit and use the following instructions to make your own:

Using a drill press and a bit that's appropriate for the material, drill a hole through your chosen object from top to bottom. Purchase a cap and a base that complement the chosen object, checking that they are big enough to cover the drilled holes. Stack the components, following the lamp kit instructions; the rod should screw into the metal components and recess $\frac{1}{4}$" from the bottom of the base. If the base has feet, the cord can be left loose; if not, drill an exit hole in the base. Insert the rod through the base, the drilled object, and the cap, securing the cap and base with washers.

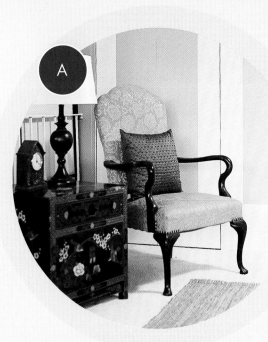

element complements the new bamboo shades and contrasts with the smooth wood furnishings.

Next, the dresser is positioned beneath the wall of windows, leaving an existing chair and chest embellished with traditional Chinese motifs to form a cozy sitting area. The curvy lines of the chair contrast well with the hard edges of the furnishings and nearby closet doors. The golden upholstery on the chair is right at home against the green walls and gold-painted closet doors.

To give purpose to the bare corner opposite the bed and to fill a need in the room, a tall freestanding mirror is added. The piece consists of an inexpensive unframed mirror and

shades that contrast nicely with the dark wood furnishings. The natural texture of the bamboo blends well with the overall Asian feel. Above the shades hang three custom-made cornice boxes. The structure and strong lines of the boxes are reminiscent of the lines on the closet doors and furnishings; painted the same color as the walls, the boxes create a striking focal point that couldn't have been achieved with ordinary valances. Gold-painted detail molding on the face of each box provides additional visual interest and dimension.

To round out the lighting pool, two new lamps are created for the space. Fashioned from pieces of stripped and brightly painted firewood, white barrel shades, and simple black

To make better use of the space at the foot of the bed, a tufted fabric bench is added to give the homeowners a place to rest and comfortably change footwear—and it provides a luxurious touch.

fluted casing stained in a dark tone to complement the other furnishings in the room.

Finally, new accessories pull the room together. Plastic ivy and baskets once hung on a ceiling beam. Now the beams are bare, and the room has thoughtfully chosen, pared-down decorative touches, including dark-tone clocks and photo frames.

Bright Lighting Ideas

This room had the advantage of large windows, but covered with dark wood blinds, they weren't attractive. To soften the look, the windows are now dressed with light-tone bamboo

bases, the new lamps contrast with the strong lines of the furnishings, ceiling beams, and cornice boxes. The red paint provides a bold pop of color against the green wall.

Ⓐ The existing upholstered chair and the chest with Asian motifs create a cozy reading area near the closets.

Ⓑ Kristan and Dave collaborated on this cushy bench; the red provides a burst of color against the warm greens and yellows present throughout the room.

CORNICE BOX

A cornice box is a great alternative to a valance. The three custom cornice boxes in this room are painted to match the wall color; a complementary gold color is used on decorative molding that adds some interesting dimension to the boxes. These instructions are for a basic cornice box that can be painted, covered with fabric, or treated with decorative molding or trim. If you are hanging curtain panels, shades, or another window treatment behind the cornice box, mount the hardware for the treatment before installing the cornice box.

C For an additional burst of color—and visual depth to each architectural cornice box—Dave chose to attach thin pieces of gold-painted molding to the face of each box.

You Will Need

2x4 board

Lightweight ¾" medium-density fiberboard (MDF)

Tape measure, pencil

Circular saw

Drill, drill bits, screws

1 Measure the width of the window frame, subtract 1 inch, and rip the 2x4 board to this width. This will be the mounting board for the cornice box.

2 Cut the MDF for each piece of the box: the box front (the window width x the box height), the top (the window width x 4 to 5 inches), and the two sides (4 to 5 inches wide x the height of the box minus ¾ inch for a perfect fit with the top). The box front can be cut to any height desired, but a height of less than 8 inches is not recommended (consider the height and size of your individual window for best proportions).

3 Attach the two sides to the top, ensuring the pieces are flush and square. Attach the front of the box to the sides and top.

4 Determine where to place the cornice box on the wall; mark the top edge on the wall (Photo A). Center the cut piece of 2x4 about ½ inch below the mark; attach the board to the wall with the wide side of the board against the wall.

5 Attach the box to the mounting board (Photo B).

PILLOWS ⓵⓪⓵

One of the least expensive, most versatile decorating elements is the pillow. A grouping of pillows can instantly change the feel of a room, not just bedrooms. On a traditional-style dark neutral sofa, a plethora of pillows in muted plaids, prints, and contrasting solids gives the sofa—and the room—a solid, traditional feel. Toss on some bright pillows with geometric prints,

Ⓐ

Ⓐ Old pants become comfy places to lie on the floor and watch TV when cut open, restitched, and stuffed with large pillow forms. See page 122 for this room.

and the same room looks contemporary. Barkcloth and other heavily textured fabrics on the pillows would give the room an exotic African ambience.

Start by choosing colors that you want to accentuate in the room: the red from a framed print, the yellow from the window treatments, or the green from the rug, for example. Ratchet up the color a bit; go one shade darker or brighter rather than trying for an exact match. Use some patterns too. Bold stripes, pastoral toiles, sweet florals, contemporary geometrics, or whatever complements the look of your room can have more impact than solid colors.

Consider the living room on pages 18 to 25: The bold geometry of the sofa pillows mimics the nautical-style grommet-top window treatment. By combining two squares and a rectangle in a palette of the room colors, the pillows

also give the traditionally shaped sofa a modern feel, so it blends into the room.

Think beyond the typical one-size square. One of the larger Western states could probably be covered with just all 12- or 14-inch-square pillows resting on sofas across the country. That's a shame, because pillows come in an endless variety of shapes. Consider using tiny square pillows, big and deep floor pillows, long

Making Pillows

Making basic square pillows is quick and easy—no sewing machine is required. To make a basic square pillow, purchase a pillow form in the desired size. Cut two pieces of fabric to the dimensions of the pillow, adding ½ inch to each dimension. Put the fabric pieces right sides together and either stitch three sides together or use fusible hem tape. Turn right side out and put the pillow form inside. Then sew tiny stitches with an invisible (monofilament) thread or use more fusible hem tape to close the opening. Alternatively, you can also close the opening with easy-to-apply snaps.

B Stacks of plump pastel-print pillows—in stripes, florals, and solids—promote the cottage style of this bedroom and comfort. See page 110 for this room.

rectangular pillows, or hexagonal pillows to add visual interest to any room.

In kids' rooms and other casual spaces, use pillow shapes and fabrics to establish a playful atmosphere. And, in rooms where children play and lie on the floor, use floor pillows. They provide extra ground-level seating for parties, TV viewing, and lounging around the family room. The pants-covered body pillows *left* (and on pages 122 to 127) show how much style floor pillows can add!

Pillows come in a nearly limitless selection of sizes, colors, and motifs. To add personal flair to a ready-made pillow, use such items as rib-bons, buttons, tassels, or beads. These inexpensive touches can easily be added with hand stitches or fusible hem tape.

Add extra pillows to a bed to plump up bedroom style. For example, a handful of pillows adds all the pattern this bedroom *above* (and on pages 110 to 115) needs. The mix of patterns and solid colors and different sizes works because the decorative style and color palette are in sync with the decor of the room.

C A bold red fabric used for the pillows adds some spice to the light-color sofa in this room. See pages 136 to 141 for this room.

REMAKE YOUR ROOMS

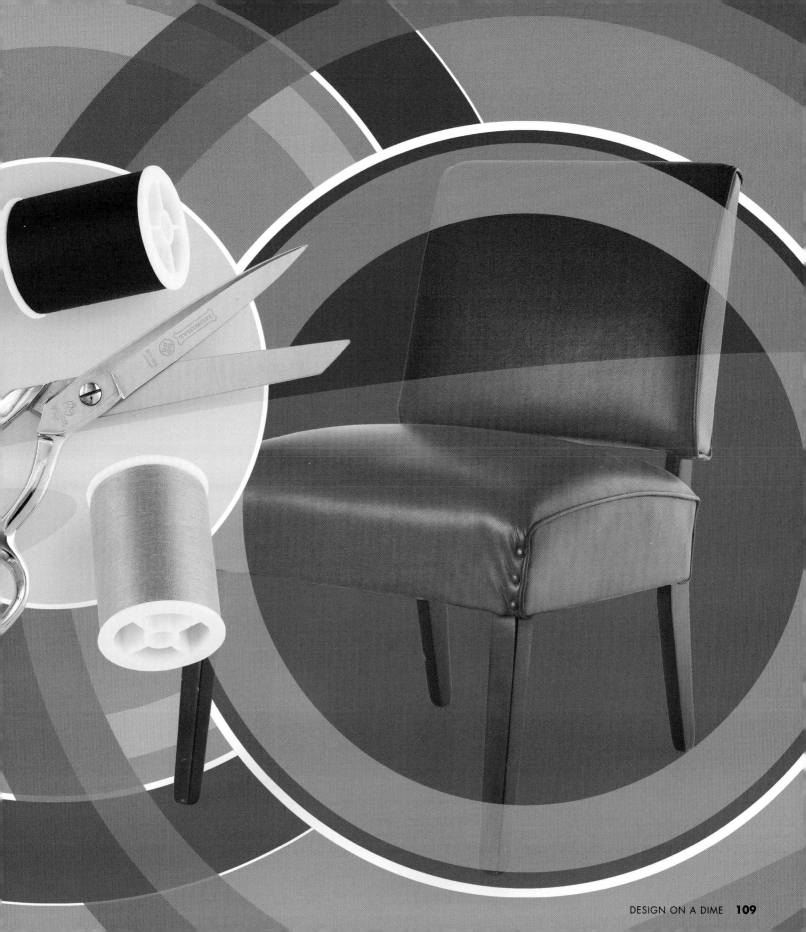

A

BEFORE

COZY AND COTTAGE STYLE

Ideally a bedroom is a retreat, an oasis from the day's stress. This bedroom housed a group of furnishings that didn't match in style or scale. Lacking color and a worthy focal point, this room was far from the cozy, romantic space the home-owners desired. If your bedroom isn't the haven you crave, follow the cues of this makeover to make your space a functional, comfortable, relaxing room that you can enjoy.

Design Team

Sam Kivett, Summer Baltzer, Charles Burbridge

The Situation

• The furnishings don't complement one another: They vary in scale, style, and wood tone.

• The room lacks color. The walls and closet doors are white, and the light green window treatments and pale patterned bedding are too timid to make an impact.

• The lighting is insufficient, with one overhead fixture and a small lamp on a nightstand in the corner of the room.

The Solutions

• A new headboard and dressers—made of knotty pine—unify the furnishings. The existing nightstands are in good condition and are in scale with the bed, so they are refurbished.

• The walls are painted a soft lilac, and the closet doors are enhanced with a calming green paint, giving the look of a country armoire. A mix of fabrics in a unified color scheme brings interest to the windows and bed.

• Additional lights are strategically placed throughout the room, including lamps on the nightstands that flank the bed and wall-mounted sconces beside the mirror.

Furniture Facelifts

Furnishings can consume a large portion of any room makeover budget. When the budget is limited—in this case, $1,000—and the furnishings need to be replaced, smart choices have to be made. Originally this room had mismatched furniture, including a bed, a tall armoire, a smaller dresser, and two nightstands. To unify the space and create a cottage-style retreat, new pieces are introduced, and some of the existing pieces are given a facelift.

First things first: the bed. Because of their importance and size, beds are natural bedroom focal points. Unfortunately, the existing bed wasn't worthy of this status: Its head- and footboard were nearly invisible, and the bedding was outdated. An unfinished headboard with simple lines and minimal ornamentation, replaces the old one;

Ⓐ A subtle mix of color, pattern, and texture brings personality to a previously bland room. Ⓑ Sconces flank the mirror to offer both lighting and a sense of style. Ⓒ Because the bed is the rightful focal point of any bedroom, a new headboard was in order in this room. Piles of pillows offer comfort and reinforce the color scheme.

B

A

The Basic Elements for the Perfect Bedroom Makeover

Are you ready to infuse your bedroom with new style but you aren't sure where to begin? *Design on a Dime's* Summer Baltzer offers these basics to keep in mind, regardless of your chosen style:

Paint. It's the easiest and most inexpensive change you can implement in a room. The great thing about paint is if you don't like the result, you can paint over it.

Window treatments. This is another inexpensive way to enhance your room. Superstores offer low-cost solutions for all types of windows, and making your own stretches your dollar even further.

Artwork. Choose artwork that not only coordinates with your new bedroom but also is meaningful to you. Don't just fill your walls for the sake of filling them: Be inspired by your pieces. To save money, you can recycle or revamp old artwork by just changing the frame or matting. You can also create your own custom artwork. Be creative!

Accessories. This is the last step in any room makeover, but it is certainly important. You can save money by shifting or recycling accessories from other rooms. You can also find great pieces at superstores and flea markets for not a lot of money.

the light-color knotty pine suits the cottage feel the homeowners desire, suits the budget, and commands attention. Flanked by the nightstands and topped with new bedding and pillows, the bed becomes a strong focal point.

Next, the two dark wood storage pieces were addressed. The tall armoire positioned opposite the bed, next to the large closet, and the shorter

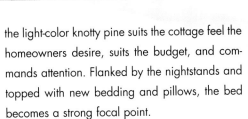

Ⓐ and Ⓒ Matching dressers take the place of an armoire, offering up just as much storage space without the visual bulk. A mirror spanning the two pieces reflects light from the windows, making the room brighter.
Ⓑ Whispy white streaks accentuate the plain flat lilac-color walls. The treatment gives the walls implied dimension.

dresser placed on the wall adjacent to the bed were unable to fit in with the new look and had to go. In their place are two matching dressers that create a more unified look. The two dressers hold as much as the armoire and the dresser combined, so storage space isn't compromised. The room size doesn't allow many furniture arrangements, so the bed remains in the original position. Placing the new dressers side by side on the wall adjacent to the bed allows space for a bench at the foot of the bed.

The bench, purchased at a thrift store for $25, is the size and scale to suit the bed. To conceal imperfections, the bench is draped with a soft lilac

BEFORE

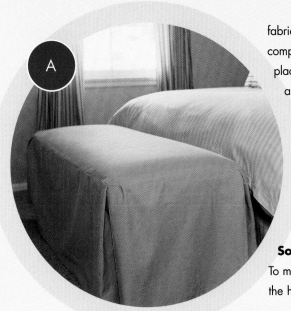

fabric that coordinates with the bedding and complements the purple walls. The bench is a place to change footwear, provides storage, and ties in with the cottage look.

Finally, the existing nightstands, whose dark finish doesn't fit the new room, are transformed with lilac and white paint and crackle medium. The new pieces complement the room and function as well as they did before.

Soft Color

To make this room a peaceful, tranquil haven for the homeowners, soft colors are chosen to cover

curtain panels hung from wood-tone rods, contributing to the hodgepodge of colors in the room. The windows are redressed with the same striped fabric of some of the pillows. The vertical stripes on the panels add height to the space; hanging the rods above the window frames contributes to the illusion of height.

Pretty Touches

To complete the makeover, cottage-style touches are added to the room. Previously the homeowners had few personal items in the room, except for some framed photos and stacks of books on the nightstands. Now additional

Bedding can be the most costly element in a bedroom makeover, but it provides much-needed focus and cohesion of color and pattern in a bedroom. —Summer Baltzer

the walls. Soothing lilac and complementary green set the tone for the cottage look and blend well with the neutral carpeting. White woodwork, the crackled nightstands, and the light wood tones of the new furnishings complete the look. To bring dimension to the walls, the homeowners applied white paint in wispy strokes.

Pattern-Perfect

With the color scheme firmly established by the wall colors, a mix of pretty fabrics in stripes, florals, and solids is introduced. On the bed, a green and white striped comforter is a perfect backdrop for plump pillows that add a touch of romance to the room. Previously, green tab-top

framed photos, seashells in a bowl, and a vase with dried lilacs pull together the colors and overall feel in the space.

To address the lighting problems, lamps with brass bases and white shades are added to the nightstands. The lamps provide light for reading in bed. The sconces that flank the mirror above the dressers provide general and accent lighting. The same brass tone of the fixtures complements the hardware of the furnishings.

Ⓐ A slipcovered thrift store find brings a bit of luxury to the room with padded seating. Ⓑ The cool green on the closet doors offers contrast to the all-lilac room and helps tie together the painted finish on the walls and the fabrics used throughout the room. The color variation also highlights the architecture and emphasizes the cottage look.

CRACKLE-FINISH FURNITURE

Crackling is a fun, exciting way to add personality to wood furniture—for little time and expense. In this room two ordinary nightstands are transformed with lilac and white paint and crackle medium. Crackling can also be used for dressers, headboards, photo frames, or anything that needs a spark of style.

Crackle medium is readily available at crafts stores and home improvement centers. When applied between a base coat and a contrasting top coat—and allowed to cure for a set amount of time—it will cause the top coat to split or crack so some of the base coat shows through. Before beginning your project, read the crackle manufacturer's directions carefully; product curing times and application methods vary by manufacturer. Some brands require two separate products, while others call for only one.

If you have never crackle-painted before, experiment with the technique on a primed piece of foam-core board, using different color combinations, thicknesses of crackle medium, and application tools (for example, paintbrushes and sea sponges). Note the methods that produce the look you want.

You Will Need

Nightstand or other wood furnishing

Sandpaper, tack cloth

Screwdriver

Flat or eggshell latex paint for top and base coats, in desired colors

Crackle medium

Paintbrushes, paint tray

Optional: Sea sponge

Optional: Water-base polyurethane

1 Remove all doors, drawers, and hardware from the piece of furniture. Lightly sand all surfaces to be painted; wipe away dust with a tack cloth.

2 Using a paintbrush apply the base coat to all surfaces; let dry. Following the manufacturer's directions, apply the crackle medium to the surfaces. Allow the medium to cure for the recommended length of time.

3 For horizontal or vertical cracks, apply top coat paint with a paintbrush, consistently brushing in one direction. For random veinlike cracks, dab on the top coat with a sea sponge. (Photos A, B, and C). Do not overlap the top coat paint application once crackling begins (this will cause the paint to lift away and smear, disturbing the crackle finish). Allow the top coat paint to dry.

4 If desired, apply an even coat of water-base polyurethane to the project surface; let dry. Reattach all hardware and reinsert any doors or drawers.

BEFORE

HARDWORKING '50s FLAIR

Whether you work out of your home or need a space for Internet surfing, your office can be a fun and stylish place to spend time. This room with hardwood floors and a lovely corner of windows had little else going for it: The desk was too small and the room was cluttered. Using the homeowner's 1950s hair dryer as inspiration, the *Design on a Dime* team created an exciting, functional space that's as hardworking as it is quirky.

Design Team

Sam Kivett, Summer Baltzer, Charles Burbridge

The Situation

• The hand-me-down desk is too small to accommodate a computer and other necessities—and its style is too traditional for the new '50s style.

• Storage space is inadequate. Paperwork, record albums, and other items are exposed on open shelving, and boxes line nearly all the walls, creating a cluttered look.

• Narrow blinds on the windows let in natural light, but they are too utilitarian.

• The room has no definite style; it contains mismatched furnishings, a record player, and a large vintage hair dryer.

The Solutions

• A retro-style desk is restored to its original condition. The large top can easily handle the computer and paperwork.

• Numerous closed storage pieces, as well as attractive bookcases, are introduced. These corral the clutter with ease.

• To dress up the windows, aluminum blinds with bright trim are hung.

• A midcentury retro-style look is established, incorporating the unusual furnishings.

Refurbished Furnishings That Fit

A home office is a work space for personal computing, sorting and paying bills, and/or participating in hobbies. Obviously, then, the first thing to consider when redoing an office is whether the work space you currently have is sufficient. In this space, the existing desk wasn't large enough to hold a computer and other office essentials. Although it had many drawers, they were all on one side and were difficult to access while seated.

To remedy the problem, a large metal desk with a laminate top, purchased at a secondhand store for $75, is selected for the room. Because the desk has some surface imperfections, it is refinished at a paint and body shop, where it is given a carlike high-gloss finish. The striking silver piece coordinates with the other metal touches in the

Ⓐ A quartet of shelves organizes formerly boxed materials in a gridlike fashion, making them easy to find. Ⓑ A restored dental cart offers extra storage and adds to the funky charm of the room. Ⓒ Wide blinds in a silver finish give great emphasis to one of the best features of the room, the wide bank of windows. The red tape is a witty accent.

room, and the large drawers are easy to reach and can store larger items than the smaller drawers in the old desk. The new desk chair is another inexpensive ($3) thrift store find.

Another refurbished piece, an old dental cart, becomes a printer table. When Charles Burbridge found the cart, it was covered with grime. To ready the cart for use in this office, it was cleaned with methyl ethyl ketone, a cleaning solvent specifically made to clean laminate tops without damaging the laminate or the adhesive that creates the bond. Finally, the drawer pulls were repainted and wheels were added, making the piece movable. This table frees up

room was cluttered because of myriad storage boxes, a record collection and record player, and other items. Although keeping the boxes in the open makes them more accessible, it isn't pleasing to the eye.

To corral the clutter, a few new furnishings are brought into the room. First, four slim bookcases, positioned to face the desk, hold important items that need to be within easy reach. To bring some personality into the space, the bookcases also display photographs. Second, to hold a prized record collection and to display a turntable, a white credenza with metal accents is introduced. The

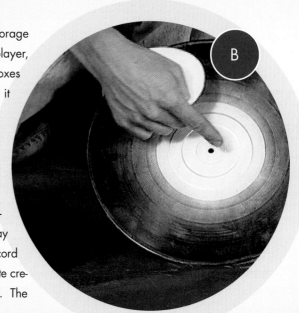

If you are high-stress when working in your office, choose cool, relaxing blues, greens, and purples for the walls. If you tend to procrastinate, use warm red, yellow, or orange to energize your work session. —Lee Snijders

valuable desk space that the printer would otherwise occupy, and the additional drawers keep items off the floor and concealed from view.

Originally, all the furnishings were against the walls. To bring attention to the new desk, it is angled in a corner. With the windows behind, a cozy, inviting space is created. The printer cart is positioned between the wall and the desk; it can easily be moved to accommodate a different arrangement.

Storage Solutions

If a desk is the main feature of an office, storage comes in a close second. All too often, offices become dumping grounds for office essentials—anything resembling paperwork—and items that don't have a home elsewhere. This

attractive piece lends itself to the look of the room while orderly stashing the records.

Custom Touches: A Nod to the 1950s

The homeowner's 1950s hair dryer inspired the theme for this room makeover, which is carried out thoroughly with vintage furnishings and a

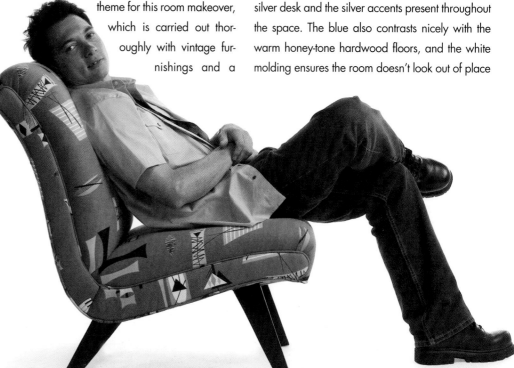

retro color palette. The walls were previously a blank white slate; now they are dressed in aqua blue, nearly the same color as the popular '57 Chevy. The cool blue is a great backdrop for the white credenza and hair dryer, not to mention the silver desk and the silver accents present throughout the space. The blue also contrasts nicely with the warm honey-tone hardwood floors, and the white molding ensures the room doesn't look out of place

Ⓐ A white metal credenza matches the attitude of the metal desk and dental cart. Above the turntable, painted record albums highlight the retro music theme. Ⓑ Pop music becomes pop art when old vinyl albums are painted silver and red and hung on the wall. Start by painting the center sections silver; then mask them off and spray the remainder red.

when viewed from an adjacent room. The lesson: If you paint a room in a color that's wildly different from the others in your home, unify the spaces with a common color, such as painted molding.

The classic aluminum blinds represent the 1950s better than a valance or full-length curtain panels would. To further bring classic '50s style into the room, a pair of chrome hubcaps is fashioned into a one-of-a-kind light fixture to replace the Victorian-style fixture that barely illuminated the space. Small lamps on the desk and credenza add task lighting.

Finally, red-hot accents enter the room via a photo frame on the desk, twill tape bands on the blinds, and painted record albums arranged above the credenza. The records are painted silver in the center and red on the outer portion. The albums provide a splash of warm color against the icy walls, heating up the space in small doses.

A A retro hair dryer becomes instant sculpture in a room infused with '50s style. **B** Aqua brings to mind other icons of a previous era—poodle skirts, saddle shoes, hot rods, and rock and roll. It sets the tone for fun, and the rest of the room reflects that mood. Touches of red add a hot contrast.

HUBCAP LIGHT FIXTURE

Rev up your lighting with a fun and funky hubcap chandelier. Summer found a pair of hubcaps—which perfectly suit the '50s look the *Design on a Dime* team was after—at a store specializing in vintage auto parts. (She paid $50.) When hung one over the other and placed over the existing lightbulb assembly, the hubcaps gave a hot retro look overhead.

When purchasing the components for this project, keep the following in mind: You will need two hubcaps, a smaller, deeper one to fit against the ceiling and a larger one to hang beneath the first. After purchasing the hubcaps and positioning them for hanging, cut the ball chain to the desired length. Ball chain couplers are available where ball chain is sold; the clasp that joins two ball chains is on one end and a loop is on the other. Check that the loop is large enough to accommodate the chain. Finally, turn off the electricity at the main breaker before doing any wiring.

Obviously we can't bring an entire car in here, so we're bringing in the hubcaps instead. —Summer Baltzer

You Will Need

2 vintage or reproduction hubcaps
Ball chain, 4 ball chain couplers slightly larger than the ball chain
Electric drill, assorted metal drill bits
Existing chandelier assembly, or lamp assembly kit
Ceiling chandelier bracket with screws for holding the light assembly
All-thread pipe (also called lamp pipe) or precut lamp pipe with both ends threaded
Lightbulb assembly for holding bulbs in a horizontal position
2 locknuts, 2 decorative locknuts (preferably chrome); optional: hacksaw

1 Drill a hole in the center of the small hubcap large enough to receive the lamp pipe. Drill two holes opposite each other in the hubcap rim to receive ceiling mount screws. Drill four equidistant holes in the rim of the smaller hubcap to accommodate the ball chain. Drill four matching equidistant holes in the tabs of the larger (lower) hubcap.

2 Attach a coupler to one end of one chain; run the other end through the hole in one of the tabs and through the loop of the coupler, forming a loop. Run the chain through the matching hole in the smaller hubcap; draw the chain across the back of the hubcap to the next hole and down through that hole. Slip the loop of the coupler over the chain; then slip the chain end through the hole in the tab of the lower hubcap. Clip the coupler in place to form a second hanging loop. Repeat for the opposite side of the hubcaps.

3 Remove the old fixture, keeping the bulb fixture and pipe in place if possible. If using an existing chandelier assembly, put the pieces back together in the original order. If building a new assembly, follow these directions: Mount the chandelier bracket assembly to the ceiling. If necessary, cut the all-thread pipe to fit between the hubcaps and into the top hubcap. Run the pipe into the upper hubcap; secure it with a locknut. Place a second locknut on the outside of the hubcap. Run the wires of the lightbulb assembly through the pipe; screw the lightbulb assembly to the remaining end of the lamp pipe.

4 Rewire the chandelier wires to the ceiling wires. Slip the holes of the upper hubcap over the screws of the ceiling bracket. Secure the upper hubcap to the ceiling with decorative locknuts.

BEFORE

FUN (FOR) THE FAMILY

True family rooms need to be versatile: Adults and children use the space for various activities, from watching TV and playing to reading and entertaining. Keeping these needs in mind is important when designing a family-friendly space. If you desire a fun, functioning space for your family to enjoy together and aren't sure how to pull it together, consider the changes made to this room as a starting point.

Design Team

Sam Kivett, Summer Baltzer, Charles Burbridge

The Situation

• This room needs to accommodate many activities. However, the arrangement of the furnishings is haphazard. Dining occurs at a coffee table in front of the TV.

• This space doesn't have enough storage units for games, toys, and video equipment; these items are stored in plastic bins that are scattered around the room.

• The two young children who live in this home are budding artists, but they don't have a place where they can display their work.

• There is insufficient lighting.

The Solutions

• The room is rearranged into two separate areas: a living room and a dining space, complete with a new table and four chairs.

• The unattractive bins are removed. A pair of bookcases hold videos, and a custom toy box corrals toys and games.

• Artwork and photographs are showcased in custom frames and on a large magnetic board.

• Floor and table lamps and hanging fixtures properly illuminate the space.

Designed for the Whole Family

To make the space suitable for multiple activities, the room arrangement needed to be addressed. The homeowners had a nice pair of '50s-style leather sofas; however, positioned on opposite ends of the room, the sofas didn't lend themselves to conversation. Because these pieces are in good condition, they are repositioned adjacent to each other (one taking the place of a piano that's been moved to another room) to create an intimate area for conversation or reading. Anchored by the existing red Oriental rug, the sofas have definite purpose, defining the "living" portion of the room.

To further define the living area, a trifold screen, taken from another room in the house, is introduced. Positioned behind one of the sofas, it eliminates the need for additional art-

Ⓐ Divide the room and conquer the clutter by creating distinct zones for different activities. Ⓑ The old floor pillows were worn beyond repair; worn pants still serve a purpose, taking on new life when stuffed and recycled into cushions. Ⓒ Small matching bookcases organize videos and books and offer display space on top.

work and adds coziness to the space. Two short bookcases line the wall where a sofa once stood. The shelves hold a collection of videotapes and books, and the tops display flowers and a lamp, which provides good ambient lighting. A floor lamp is added between the two sofas for soft illumination.

Because the family enjoys spending time on the floor—playing, reading, and watching TV—floor pillows are added to the space. Two large minimum-sew pillows are created from a funky pair of plaid pants and a pair of jeans purchased at a secondhand store—a great way to reuse discarded items for decorative purposes.

mulating too many toys or losing toys at the bottom of the box.

A Place to Dine

Previously, this multipurpose room didn't have a proper table and seating for dining. The family sat on the floor on pillows to dine at a coffee table. To get the family off the floor, a new table is positioned adjacent to the kitchen, defining an eating area and offering a place for adults to sit comfortably and keep an eye on what's happening in the living room. The sturdy unfinished table and chairs were purchased for less than $300; with a coat

> *When decorating a room where children are involved, it's always important to add a few elements that are made specifically for them.* —Summer Baltzer

Finally, to corral clutter, a small lidded toy box, painted the same color as the walls, stands next to one sofa. This box keeps toys off the floor when they're not in use, promotes picking up, and, because of its size, discourages accu-

of dark stain they complement other dark wood tones in the room.

To make the table multipurpose, a wide roll of butcher paper is rigged to the underside of one end with rope, a conduit pipe, and S hooks. When pulled and stretched across the tabletop, it creates a canvas on which the children can doodle while dinner is prepared.

With all the activities that occur at the table, proper illumination is key. Initially, no lighting served the space now occupied by the table, so a pair of hanging pendants was added. In addition, the attractive corner windows near the table—formerly covered with long white tab-top curtains—are now covered with light-filtering matchstick blinds. The look complements the

---

Making a Room Family-Friendly

Accommodating people of different ages—and sizes—is a consideration when planning a common area in a home. Dave Sheinkopf offers these great ideas for turning a living room into a family oriented space:

Choose furniture that reflects the family and the activities they perform. Soft, comfy sofas are great for some, while some might prefer more structured traditional pieces.

Think safety. When small children are present, prevent corners, such as those on tables, from being a hazard by rounding or padding them.

Use lighting to perfect the space. A combination of table, floor, and overhead lighting suits many different activities.

Ⓐ Moving the sofas so they cuddle up together creates an intimate area for family activities. Keeping the floor space open lets the family sprawl out for games and playtime. Ⓑ A small toy chest doubles as an end table and keeps the clutter under cover. Painting it to match the walls keeps it from being conspicuous.

A

Using acid-free materials is very important for preserving any artwork. —Charles Burbridge on using archival-quality materials for custom-framing projects

wall color and furnishings and adds a bit of natural texture to the space.

Artwork Showcase
Family rooms are ideal places to feature the artwork of young family members. To call attention to some special pieces in this room, they are enclosed in deep-set, black-painted frames that are hung above the television. The artwork is attached to backing material with acid-free double-sided tape to preserve and protect it from yellowing and deterioration—an important consideration for any artwork.

To provide a display space where artwork can be changed and moved around on a whim, a large magnetic board is positioned behind the dining table. This exciting focal point is created from tin. Framed with narrow strips of wood trim painted green (a shade darker than the walls for subtle emphasis), this custom-made display board costs much less than a similar-

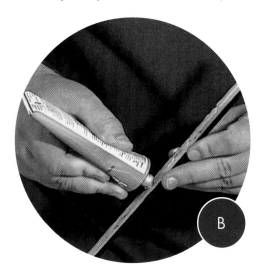

B

C

A Gleaming metal makes a stylish backing for framed children's artwork. B Charles creates a custom frame by gluing wood trim to the metal backing. C Double-sided acid-free tape is used to adhere the artwork to the metal backing; the tape is archival-quality, so it won't cause the artwork to deteriorate the way regular adhesive tape would.

size ready-made magnetic board would. For an even easier option, look for specially formulated magnetic paint at paint stores and home improvement centers. For added color, magnetic paint can usually be covered with latex paint. Another option is chalkboard paint, available in cans and in spray form, in black and green.

TABLETOP CANVAS

No need for an easel—this great project makes any tabletop a temporary canvas for drawing and painting. Materials are readily available at a hardware store and kitchen supply warehouse. For little expense or effort, you'll get a disposable surface than can protect the permanent one underneath.

D With only a few materials, turn any tabletop into a canvas for a budding artist.

You Will Need
Table
Butcher paper roll
S hooks, eye-hooks, fender washers, nuts (2 of each)
Electrical conduit slightly longer than length of butcher paper roll
Rope
Drill, drill bit

1 On the underside of the table, drill two holes 2 inches from the edge (Photo A).

2 Insert an eye-hook into each hole; secure each hook with a washer and nut on the tabletop. Hang an S hook from each eye-hook (Photo B).

3 Thread rope through the electrical conduit. Thread the conduit through the paper roll (Photo C).

4 Secure each end of the rope to the S hooks with a knot.

For a video demonstration of this project and more *Design on a Dime* ideas, visit HGTV.com/dod

OVERHEAD LIGHTING ⓵⓪⓵

One central overhead light is often the only hardwired lighting fixture in a room. As the *Design on a Dime* teams often demonstrate, a single ceiling fixture doesn't light a room evenly and is rarely placed in the right spot for the furnishings. At the other extreme, rooms that have no central light fixture usually lack sufficient illumination for the tasks and activities

that take place in the room. An overhead light source often creates a good lighting scheme, which usually includes floor and table lamps for a balance of general, ambient, and task lighting. Here are examples of *Design on a Dime* turning mundane into magnificent for little expense.

Take Cues from the Decor

A room so wonderfully and completely representative of a style (in this case, Asian, in the room *opposite top* and on pages 62 to 69) deserves a light fixture that stays on message. To add evenly soft light to this room, paper lanterns in a variety of sizes are strung from a bamboo grid. Because there is no electrical connection in the ceiling, the cord is hidden in the frame, which extends all the way to the wall. The dark wall color and strategically placed artwork disguise the remaining cord.

Ⓐ Three custom fixtures take the place of one odd-placed light source in this dining room. See page 72 for this room.

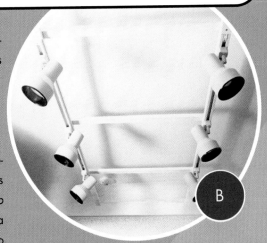

Ⓑ Track light fixtures are great for kitchens because they can be positioned to illuminate any specific area, such as a countertop or stovetop. See page 86 for this room.

Lighting for Dining

Ceiling lights in dining rooms may not hang directly over the dining table. Because of built-in cabinets, storage pieces, or taking advantage of a view from a window, a table may not be perfectly centered in a room. Moving and rewiring a ceiling fixture is a major job, so consider using the existing wiring and adjusting the placement of the fixture. Using multiple lights coming from a

C Rely on the *Design on a Dime* team for innovative solutions, such as this bamboo grid and pattern lantern fixture. See page 62 for this room.

central line allows you to direct the light wherever you want it, as shown in the room *opposite far left* and on pages 72 to 79.

When buying light fixtures, consider how they look when they are not lit. Chandeliers, for example, sparkle in whatever light reaches the room (for instance, sunlight from windows or light cast from the next room), so they brighten a space even when they are off. The inverted copper pot *right* (and on pages 136 to 141) has the same effect, with a delightful and singular twist. More appropriate in this room than a sparkling chandelier, the smooth and textured copper surfaces gleam and shimmer.

Lighting Is Key in Kitchens

Good lighting is essential in a kitchen. Incorporating a balanced lighting scheme into an existing kitchen can be expensive. The rack of directional lights *opposite left* (and on pages 86 to 91) greatly improves the livability of this kitchen for little expense. The light is more evenly distributed for general lighting, and the lights drop several inches from the ceiling to light work surfaces for task lighting.

D Nearly any object, such as a copper pot, can become an overhead light fixture with the help of an easy-to-find and -use lighting kit. See page 136 for this room.

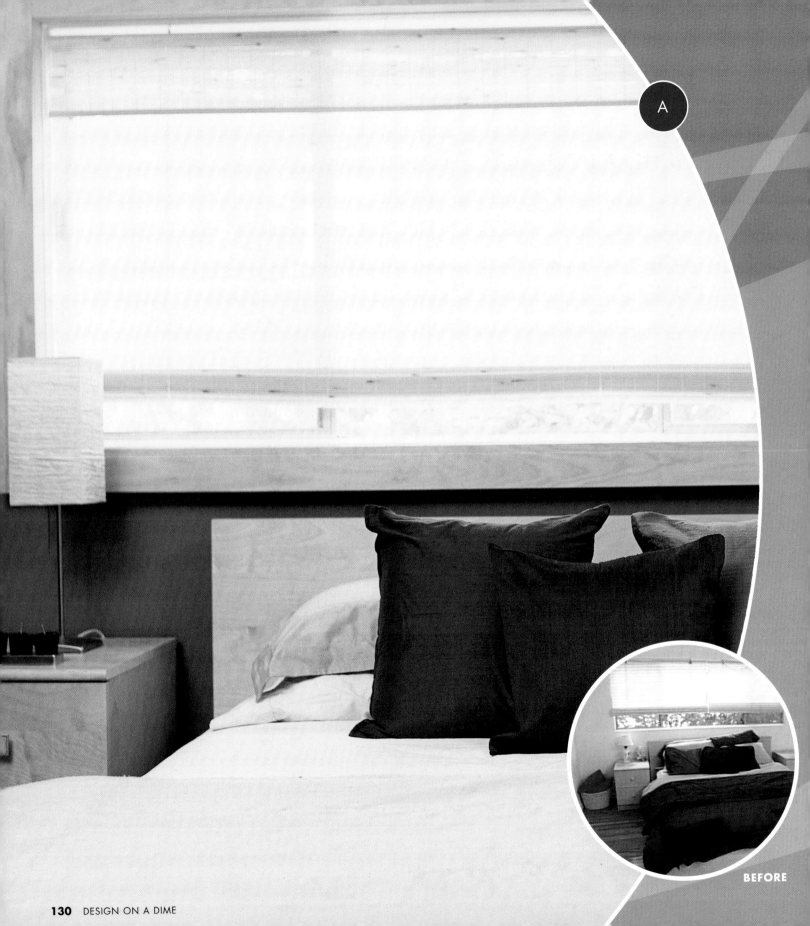

A

BEFORE

TRANQUIL RETREAT ⟨WITH⟩ ASIAN FLAIR

Sometimes a room has all the essentials to function well—in this case, a bedroom with a bed, nightstands, a storage trunk, and beautiful hardwood floors—yet lacks a cohesive style to pull it all together. Further, when a room has ample space, as this one does, the function can be stretched to include more than one activity. If you have an ordinary bedroom that you want to turn into a private oasis, take cues from this dramatic makeover.

Design Team

Lee Snijders, Summer Baltzer, Charles Burbridge

The Situation

• This room is a large white box with few architectural details and no definite style.

• The low platform bed, framed by a row of windows, has the potential to be a focal point but fails to make a strong statement.

• The space isn't utilized to its full potential; there is plenty of room opposite the bed to introduce additional furnishings and make the space more than a bedroom.

The Solutions

• To bring life into this space, the walls are painted a rich orange, and the closet doors are treated to a linen look, creating instant impact.

• The bed, flanked by the existing nightstands, is now dressed in raw silk bedding and stacks of pillows. To bring attention to the bed, the window above is framed in light-color wood and covered with long matchstick blinds.

• Making use of the floor space in this room, a reading nook—complete with a banana palm wing chair, the homeowner's green distressed trunk, and a tall floor lamp—is added opposite the bed.

Color Sets the Mood

To turn this room into the get-away-from-it-all retreat the homeowner desires, the first step is to cover the stark white walls with some soothing color. To suit the chosen Asian theme—which was already firmly established with the low profile bed and clean-lined nightstands—an earthy orange now covers the walls. The rich color complements the light-tone wood floor and furnishings and allows the furnishings to take center stage. Splashes of warm color—such as the red pillows—add a dash of spice.

The painted linen treatment on the closet doors is another exciting use of color. Previously, the white doors blended into the white walls; now, however, the closet doors are a focal point, remade with brown paint a touch lighter than the surrounding walls.

Ⓐ Matchstick blinds give the window a warm tone. Together the bed and window make a strong focal point. Ⓑ Rope handles give the existing trunk a well-traveled look and help it blend with the banana palm chair. Ⓒ Comfy seating, a floor lamp, and a trunk that doubles as a coffee table create an instant reading nook, making the most of a previously unused corner.

B

Dressing Up Terra-Cotta Pots

To bring a sense of serenity into this bedroom, live potted plants are introduced. Their natural flowing lines contrast with the crisp, clean lines of the furniture, shadow box window frame, and lampshades. Because the budget is limited, expensive decorative pots are not an option; instead, ordinary terra-cotta pots are enhanced with a mixture of paint and glazing medium. The paint/glaze mixture is brushed on in a casual, loose manner for a wispy appearance. Finally, once the paint/glaze mixture is dry, a coat of water-base polyurethane is brushed on for protection and a bit of shine.

If you have terra-cotta pots that could use some excitement, keep the following in mind:

• Terra-cotta pots may be used indoors or out. For outdoor use, look for specialty patio or outdoor paints that can stand up to the elements. For indoor use, choose inexpensive acrylic paints.

• For either indoor or outdoor use, seal pots inside and out with a water-base sealer.

All Eyes on the Bed

The existing bed, set on a low platform, had the potential to become a focal point in the room: The window above had the look of a faux headboard; the flanking nightstands were the right size and proportion. However, the windows lacked attractive treatments, and the mismatched bedding had no appeal.

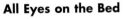

A To give texture to plain closet doors, a linen paint technique is employed. **B** The windows take on more importance when framed with wood that matches the other components of the room. **C** Previously, mismatched bedding displayed an array of competing colors. Now, luxurious raw silk in muted tones gives the room a tranquil feel.

To make the bed a proper focal point, the first step was to play up the row of windows, which provides natural light to the space. First, the windows are framed with the same light-tone wood featured throughout the room. Dressed in matchstick blinds that complement the Asian theme, the windows bring attention to the bed below.

To make the bed a restful retreat, the mismatched wintry colors and fabrics are replaced with raw silks in earth tones. The stacks of pillows and plump duvet invite slumber, and the tailored pieces show off the attractive clean lines of the head- and footboard.

Space Wise

Because the homeowner desired a spot for reading and relaxing, a reading nook is added opposite the bed. This space was vacant, except for a clothes hamper and a distressed trunk; now, a comfy banana palm wing chair stands angled in the corner. The trunk serves as a coffee table, and a floor lamp stands nearby to offer task lighting. To complete the space, two small bookcases are set against the wall opposite the chair.

Details Complete the Makeover

To bring Eastern flair into the space, decorative items, artwork, and natural elements are intro-

duced. The artwork includes a custom shadow box filled with artificial orchids and bamboo bundles, and a wood panel painted with Asian characters and splashes of warm and cool colors (now at home above the reading chair, this piece came from a nearby room). A pot with tall ferns stands behind the chair, and large daylilies flank the bookcases; the curving lines of the plants are a pleasing contrast to the straight lines of the furnishings.

Besides color and visual interest, the accessories introduce texture. The blend of natural tactile texture (the chair) and implied visual texture (the coarse woven look of the closet doors) contrasts with the smooth wood surfaces.

Ⓐ Square paper lampshades echo the shapes and textures used in the rest of the room. Ⓑ Bookcases control the clutter and anchor to a long, narrow piece of art.

LINEN PAINT TREATMENT

The look of cool, crisp linen can be duplicated with common painting tools such as glaze and a wide weaver brush—or a small inexpensive whisk broom, like the one Charles Burbridge used when he tackled this project. The resulting distinctive pattern is subtle enough to be appropriate in any room of the home. The instructions are for a large area, such as a wall; for a smaller area, such as the closet doors featured in this room, you do not need to tape off alternating sections (because you work in a small area, you can work quickly while the glaze is wet).

For this technique, a ratio of 5 parts glaze to 1 part top coat paint is a good starting point; experiment with different ratios for the look you desire. Charles used a 1:1 mixture of paint and glaze that remained from other projects.

Once again I've been faced with the dilemma of what to do with a plain white closet door. This two-coat process will simulate a woven texture much like reed or fine linen. —Charles Burbridge

You Will Need

Satin or semigloss latex paint for base and top coats in desired colors

Glaze

6-inch weaver brush

Roller and paint tray

Painter's tape

Lint-free rags

Tape measure

1 Apply the base coat to the surface; let dry. Divide the room into vertical sections, narrow enough that you can work the section from top to bottom quickly, but not so narrow that you create more seams, or vertical lines, than are visually pleasing. Using painter's tape, mask off every other section.

2 Mix 5 parts glaze to 1 part top coat paint (Photo A). Roll the glaze/paint mixture onto one section of the wall (Photo B). While the glaze is still wet, use the weaver brush to make a horizontal stripe across the top of the section (Photo C). Immediately brush in the opposite horizontal direction. Repeat, working quickly down the entire glazed section. Wipe the brush with a lint-free cloth after each stroke to remove excess glaze. Make a vertical stroke, holding the brush straight. Repeat, working quickly over the entire section.

3 Repeat the process for every masked-off section. Remove the tape; let each section dry.

4 Mask off each unpainted section, positioning the tape about ⅜ inch inside the edges of the previously painted sections. Paint the new masked-off sections with the glaze/paint mixture as described in Step 2, painting over the ⅜-inch sections to create seams. Remove the tape; let the paint dry.

A

B

C

BEFORE

ARRANGED FOR LIVING

Wide-open spaces can be difficult to design: Furnishings often line the walls, and the space isn't used to its full potential. In this long room, an abundance of natural light and beautiful hardwood floors held some promise; however, the space was void of color, and the furnishings were disorganized. By warming up the entire room and rearranging the furnishings, a functional space is created. It can now handle multiple activities and people with ease.

Design Team

Lee Snijders, Summer Baltzer, Charles Burbridge

The Situation

• The long room has ample space to accommodate living and dining activities, but the layout isn't working.

• The furnishings are mismatched; the mix includes Mission, Spanish, and contemporary pieces.

• The white walls, light-tone furnishings, and sage green sofa create a washed-out look in the room.

• Family photographs fill the space between two windows. However, mismatched frames and mats make the display a less-than-pleasing focal point.

The Solutions

• By rearranging the furnishings, two distinct areas are created.

• For a more coordinated look, the existing end table and coffee table are eliminated, and pieces that complement the dining set and sofa are introduced.

• To bring color into the space, a faux paint treatment in warm hues is applied. Touches of warm and cool colors dress up the room.

• Coordinated mats and frames unify the prized photographs.

Create a Space for Living

Before the *Design on a Dime* team tackled this transformation, the long narrow room wasn't set up to easily accommodate all the activities that occur in a living room—such as watching TV, playing games, and doing homework. The overstuffed sage green sofa was positioned along one wall, and the entertainment center stood against an adjacent wall. This arrangement didn't allow for comfortable TV viewing. The additional furnishings—a small end table and a hefty coffee table—didn't suit the space in scale or style. To make the living portion of this room more livable, it is first rearranged; then some of the old furnishings are replaced by new pieces that complement the existing sofa and desired style.

To create an intimate setting for TV viewing, the sofa is positioned to face the entertainment

Ⓐ One room easily takes on two functions when the furniture is used to define distinct spaces. Ⓑ A copper fixture centered over the dining table adds functional lighting to the area. Ⓒ Red cushions warm up the dining chairs and also add comfort, encouraging the family to linger at the table a bit longer.

A

center, putting its back to the dining table. Even with the sofa in the middle of the space, ample room remains for traffic flow and additional furnishings, including a new light-tone coffee table, a tall coordinating sofa table that stands against the long wall where the sofa used to be, and a trio of nesting tables. The nesting tables—that can actually serve as a table and chairs for the children—are personalized with a distressed paint treatment in a cool blue-green that complements the sofa and contrasts with the new wall color. Then they are stenciled with a floral motif that mimics the floral fabrics used throughout the space. Finally, a sisal rug unifies the newly designed living area.

table, the frames create a focal point in the living area. Additional framed photographs and a dried floral arrangement stand on the sofa table. The entire grouping is flanked by sconces, which provide subtle accent lighting for the photographs.

Set the Dining Room Apart

With the living room area reworked to better use the floor space, the dining area can be evaluated. The table—with a wrought-iron base in a scroll motif—and chairs are in great condition, so they are kept. Because dining space is somewhat limited, the round table suits the space better than a

Window treatments can create separate but consistent spaces. Even if different treatment styles are chosen, using the same fabric, or even coordinating fabrics, will give all the windows a sense of uniformity. —Kristan Cunningham

The wall that was filled with family photographs is also addressed. Previously, the photos were in mismatched frames and mats, and the sprawling arrangement filled the entire space between two windows. Now the photographs are grouped in uniform frames, with various mat openings accommodating different size photos. Arranged in a grid above the sofa

square or rectangular table would—another reason for maintaining the matching set. To allow more room for movement around the table, it is pulled out from the walls. The entertainment center is still in clear view from the table, in case anyone wants to watch TV while dining.

To dress up the dining set, comfy tufted red cushions are added to the chairs, and a long table runner is draped across the tabletop. The table runner fabric motif is reminiscent of the wrought-iron table base. A woven basket filled with crisp apples brings a refreshing country touch to the space.

Because the dining space lacked a light fixture overhead—needed for dining, playing board games, doing homework, and after-dinner conversation—a custom copper fixture is

Easy-to-Make Table Runner

Create a table runner—or even a fuller-coverage square or rectangular tablecloth—without sewing a stitch. Wash and dry your chosen fabric; press. Cut the fabric into the desired shape and size for your table, adding a ¼- or ½-inch seam allowance to each side. A drop of 8 inches is recommended (it won't drape onto diners seated at the table); however, it can be longer if it is used for decorative purposes (and removed for dining). Following the manufacturer's directions, use ¼- or ½-inch-wide fusible hem tape to finish the edges of the fabric.

Ⓐ Using the sofa as a room divider breaks up the big space into more usable areas without making the room feel smaller. Ⓑ Moving family photos from a hodgepodge of mismatched frames into a coordinated grid gives each picture more emphasis and makes the arrangement easier to view.

B

added. The rich copper tone of this inverted-cooking-pot-turned-light-fixture complements the wall color, and the use of metal successfully bridges the gap between country and casual-contemporary, the two looks favored in the restyled space. Finally, the rug that was beneath the table has been removed to allow for easier cleanup—a smart move, especially when children dine at the table.

A To further unite the sofa and entertainment center, a sisal rug and coffee table fill the space between the two main pieces of furniture.

B A simple-to-do rubbed wall finish repeats the rich tones of the fabrics in the room and makes the whole space feel warmer.

Unify with Color and Pattern

To make the long room feel like a unified whole—even with the distinct areas within—the walls are treated to a faux finish in warm coral and orange that heats up the entire space. The hues complement the honey-tone wood floors and set off the neutral-tone sofa as a focal point. The treatment is textural and interesting, eliminating the need for excessive wall-hung art (previously dried floral arrangements hung on the walls) yet providing an interesting backdrop for the framed photos. To further unify the space, the table runner fabric, a red and cream floral, is also used for pillows in the living area.

Arranging an Open Floor Plan

An open floor plan offers generous space, yet arranging it in a pleasing way can be challenging. Kristan Cunningham offers these ideas for making the most of an open floor plan:

Use color in fabrics and wood tones to visually connect defined areas. For interest and some degree of separation, carry a color across the space but use it in varying patterns. For example, use red striped cushions on dining chairs and red floral pillows on the sofa.

Think visual balance. Choose furnishings of roughly the same height (and in scale with one another). Hang artwork along the same center-line, regardless of the size or subject matter.

Flooring is typically the same throughout an open area, so use area rugs to group furnishings in one particular area. Use coordinating, not matching, rugs to visually tie a space together.

DISTRESSED AND STENCILED TABLES

Give a set of nesting tables a whole new look with a combination of techniques. First, sand away some of the finish for a worn, weathered look; then apply stenciling to the top. Look for precut stencils to make the detailing fast and easy. Some stencils are designed to be used in corners, and others can be easily adapted.

Ⓒ Before the top was stenciled and the base distressed, this table was a bland, unexciting piece of furniture.

You Will Need
Wooden tables

Sandpaper, tack cloth

Stencil, spray stencil adhesive, stencil brush, paper plates

Acrylic paint, in three coordinating colors

Spray varnish or sealer

Optional: soft lint-free paint rag, painter's tape

BEFORE

1 Use painter's tape to mask the tabletop (or remove it, if possible). Paint the frame of the table with one color of acrylic paint; let dry. Sand the table frame, sanding away more paint in the areas that would normally receive more wear (along edges and corners, for example). Remove sanding dust with a tack cloth.

2 Arrange the stencils on the tabletop, cutting them apart to reposition if necessary. Spray the back of the stencil with stencil adhesive, following the manufacturer's directions. Press the stencil in place. Pour a small amount of paint onto a paper plate (Photo A). Lightly dip the tip of a stencil brush in the paint. Pounce the brush on the plate to remove most of the paint so the brush is almost dry.

3 Use a scrubbing or pouncing motion to apply paint through the stencil opening, reloading the brush as needed (Photo B). Carefully remove the stencil (Photo C). Touch up ragged edges with a rag and your finger. Wash out the stencil brush and the stencil. Let the paint dry.

4 For designs with more than one stencil layer, repeat the steps to apply the stencil and paint.

5 Apply a light coat of spray varnish or sealer to the table.

TOOLS (101)

For hanging photos or creating custom furnishings, every homeowner—or renter, for that matter—needs an assortment of tools. The *Design on a Dime* team uses a variety of tools each week, selecting the best types for each and every job. Here is a rundown of some of the tools everyone needs to have on hand to tackle home improvement projects.

A The *Design on a Dime* hosts and design coordinators rely on a whole host of tools to tackle every room makeover.

Carpenter's Level. This tool is essentially a thick ruler with leveling bubbles. Hold it against the wall vertically or horizontally to determine right angles. When the bubble in the level is centered, it indicates horizontal or vertical alignment.

Chalk Line. To create a straight line to follow when painting or marking on a wall—or to find a true straight line when preparing to wallpaper—use a chalk line, a container that's filled with colored chalk and heavy string. Once a straight line is determined, snap the line; the chalk will wipe away when it's no longer needed.

Hammer. Numerous types of hammers are available. For most household use, an everyday claw hammer (that's perfect for both driving and removing nails) will work.

Handsaw/Circular Saw. Standard manual handsaws are great for ripping (cutting) lumber to the necessary width or length.

Though expensive, a circular saw is handy if you plan to construct simple furnishings or shelves—and you won't tire as quickly as you would with a handsaw.

Hot-Glue Gun and Glue Sticks. Look to crafts stores and home improvement centers for different varieties of glue guns to be used with either low- or high-temperature glue sticks. Low-

B Spencer uses a cordless drill, a wise—and not too expensive—alternative to a handheld screwdriver.

C A hot-glue gun—along with low- and high-temperature glue sticks—is a great tool to add to your toolbox. Kristan uses one with low-temperature glue sticks, which are ideal for adhering delicate materials to a surface.

temperature adhesives are preferred for bonding lightweight items, and high-temperature adhesives may be used to adhere items to metal, wood, and nonporous surfaces.

Pliers. Various types of pliers tackle different jobs. Slip-joint and needle-nose are two of the most common types. Slip-joint pliers are all-purpose pliers that easily hold and bend objects. Needle-nose pliers have a tapered end that allows you to reach into enclosed areas to bend or hold wire.

Sandpaper/Power Sander. For small jobs (smoothing tabletop edges, for example), sandpaper of various grits will suffice. For bigger jobs, or if you plan to do more serious woodworking, invest in a power sander. Orbital sanders work in a circular motion, reducing noticeable marks on wood. They can be used both with and against the grain.

Screwdriver/Cordless Drill. Handheld screwdrivers, both slotted and phillips, are used for setting or removing screws of various sizes. To reduce fatigue—and more easily set screws into nearly any material—have a cordless drill on hand.

Staple Gun. Manual staple guns can accommodate staples of varying lengths. This tool is especially handy for upholstery projects (re-covering drop-in seats, for example).

Stud Finder. This handheld device senses metal in walls, alerting you to stud locations—an important thing to know when you want to securely fasten artwork or shelving to the walls.

Tape Measure. Available in various lengths, retractable tape measures allow you to measure almost any material with ease.

Wrenches (adjustable, combination, and pipe). A standard adjustable wrench will accommodate nuts and bolts of multiple sizes. A combination wrench has an open end and a closed end that are both the same size; the closed end offers greater control and less slippage. Larger pipe wrenches are used to tighten or loosen plumbing fittings.

RESTYLE (YOUR) ROOMS

BEFORE

SO-SO TO SOPHISTICATED

Young couples are often faced with a mix of furnishings from their single days. A grouping of hand-me-downs can be difficult to coordinate, especially when the pieces are of different styles and finishes. The owners of this bedroom were faced with this situation, in addition to a lack of storage space and dated floral bedding. Fortunately, the *Design on a Dime* team was ready to help, offering great ideas to transform this cold, empty room into a stylish retreat.

Design Team

Lee Snijders, Summer Baltzer, Charles Burbridge

The Situation

• This small room is filled with mismatched furnishings, including an Asian-style screen and dark-stained wood pieces of various styles.

• The bed isn't a commanding focal point.

• With only one tiny closet, this room requires additional storage options.

• The windows are covered with utilitarian blinds, and the floral-motif bedding dominates the room.

• The white walls are uninspired.

The Solutions

• To unify the space, many of the furnishings are removed; they are replaced with sleek coordinating pieces in a dark stain. Refurbished thrift store chairs are also introduced.

• The bed is given a style boost with a padded headboard.

• A large dresser that suits the new cosmopolitan style is added to the room.

• A luxurious quilted fabric is used to dress the windows and bed (a custom duvet cover and stacks of pillows).

• A soft tan is chosen for the walls; the color is subtle, so the furnishings take center stage.

Focus on Furniture

This bedroom, with lots of windows and beautiful hardwood floors, was previously home to a mismatched grouping of furnishings: a bed sans headboard, nightstands of different styles, an Asian-style folding screen, a trunk, and a mirror and three small tables positioned along a wall opposite the bed. To unify the space and expand storage options, a large dresser and coordinating nightstands are introduced. These pieces have clean lines and dark finishes—fitting additions to a room that's destined for a rich cosmopolitan look.

To make the bed a fitting focal point, it is treated to a dark-stained headboard with a tufted fabric inset. Because the dresser and nightstands consumed a large portion of the $1,000 budget, the headboard was salvaged from a thrift store. This basic

A Placing the bed under the long window pulls together the two strongest elements in the room and creates a powerful focal point. **B** Quilted fabrics and stacked pillows add luxury and textural interest. **C** Antique and reproduction accessories carry out the upscale retro theme of the room.

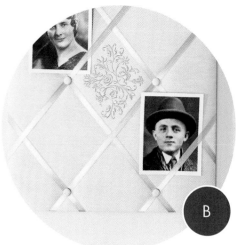

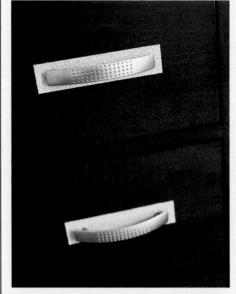

Furniture Hardware

Hardware can be more than a utilitarian feature on furnishings and cabinets—some consider it furniture jewelry! Visit any home improvement center or online resource, and you will be amazed by the variety available, from plain round ceramic or wood knobs to more elaborate brushed-metal designs. If you aren't ready to invest in new hardware, you can easily update what you have with paint and decorative techniques such as stenciling.

piece is spiffed up with the inset, created from plywood, batting, and a supple quilted fabric tufted with buttons. This is an inexpensive way to add style and bring attention to the bed, the most important furnishing in the room.

Finally, the existing mirror is retained. It's joined by two refurbished thrift store chairs that are perfect for changing footwear or lounging. The chairs are painted with the same tan paint used on the walls and then coated with polyurethane for durability; then the backs and seats are re-covered with the same quilted fabric that's used throughout the room. These newly transformed chairs prove that minimal money

and effort can turn something ordinary into extraordinary.

A Neutral Palette Sets the Mood

Although the new furnishings bring an air of sophistication to this bedroom, the color palette is the foundation for the new style. Previously,

---

A Large spaces demand furniture of similar proportions. The previous trio of tables seemed to float about unanchored. The new dresser looks right at home. **B** The color and diamond-grid pattern of a padded memory board are subtly tied to the fabrics used in the bed linens and headboard. **C** Placing bands of decorator fabric only at the top and bottom of the draperies holds down cost while keeping up style.

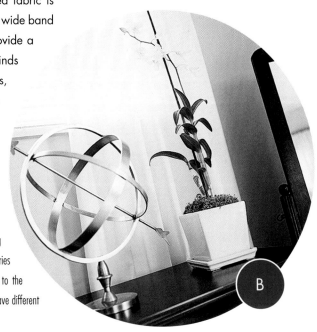

the walls were white, and the only punch of color in the room came from the bold floral bedding. First, the walls are painted a soft tan that allows the furnishings to take center stage. The light color also visually expands the space while warming it in a way white couldn't. Then, soft neutral cream floods the room—from the bedding to the windows and chairs—in luxurious quilted fabric and solid bedsheets.

A duvet cover and flange-edge pillows bring an elegant touch to the bed. The duvet cover, complete with tailored piping trim, features decorator fabric for the top and an inex-

privacy, the new window treatments frame the bed, heightening its focal-point status.

Refined Touches Ground the Room

To infuse this restyled room with an Art Deco look, a few stylish accents are introduced. First, the new dresser and nightstands are given a subtle yet effective facelift with new hardware. The original pulls and handles were too traditional to suit the new look; now, clean-lined brushed-silver hardware dresses up the furnishings. Even the windows get in on the style: The rods are brushed metal with transparent glass finials. Sophisticated touches enter the room via a

The window treatments provide a romantic alternative to the officelike blinds that previously covered the windows, and the use of sheets is a thrifty way to save money on ready-mades, which can be expensive.

Easy Ways to Make a Bed a Focal Point

The bed is the most essential piece of furniture in a bedroom: Besides sleeping on it, most people read and relax on it too. Because beds are so large, they create an obvious focal point in a room; therefore, it's important to make them attractive with interesting bedding, a sweeping canopy, or some other treatment. *Design on a Dime's* Spencer Anderson offers these great ideas for bringing attention to a bed:

Choose an interesting headboard—something with texture and color—that will draw your eye right to the bed.

Make the bed the first thing you see in the room.

Focus on the bedding. Give the bedding the biggest color punch in the room. Make it stand out or "pop" against the backdrop. Extra pillows and layered bed linens also draw the eye to the bed.

Placing an area rug under the bed can be very useful in capturing the eye.

If all else fails, make your bed into a fort using pillows and sheets. It's fun and rejuvenating!

pensive king-size bedsheet for the bottom. Forgoing decorator fabric on the back eliminates nearly half the potential cost. Secured at the top with buttons, the cover can be removed in a snap for laundering.

The windows are home to another nifty treatment: King-size bedsheets are used for the main portion of each panel, and the quilted fabric is present in a narrow band at top and a wide band at bottom. The window treatments provide a romantic alternative to the officelike blinds that previously covered the windows, and the use of sheets is a thrifty way to save money on ready-mades, which can be expensive (especially when created from quality fabrics). Besides controlling light and offering

brushed-silver and glass lamp base and an antique-style telephone on the nightstands, a silver photo frame, the armilary sphere, and a white orchid (the orchid provides a natural touch and flowing lines that contrast with the crisp edges of the furnishings and the distinct grid pattern on the quilted fabrics).

A Tiny details such as an unusual rod and finial have a big impact, giving the room updated style. **B** Paring down to a minimum of materials ties disparate accessories together. The brushed-chrome armilary sphere relates to the drawer pulls, lamp, and drapery rod. These elements have different styles but share a common material—metal.

BASIC DUVET COVER

The duvet (French for comforter) is becoming a popular alternative to standard printed or solid-color comforters. Typically, duvets are made of a cotton covering over down or feathers. Duvet covers come in nearly every color, style, and printed motif imaginable and are often expensive. Count on the *Design on a Dime* team for an inexpensive solution!

This duvet cover has a luxurious fabric for the top and an ordinary bedsheet as the backing; button closures make the cover easy to remove for laundering.

Detail Piping

Although the instructions *right* are for a duvet cover without piping, you can add this detail with $^9/_{32}$-inch cording and a zipper foot. Cut enough 1½-inch-wide bias fabric strips to equal the sides and bottom of the duvet; stitch the strips together to make one long strip. Fold and pin the long strip around the cording, matching long raw fabric edges. With the zipper foot and matching thread, stitch through the fabric layers close to the cording. Follow Step 3 to layer the fabric and bedsheet. Align the covered cording along the layered edges, cording toward the center. Continue with Steps 3 to 5 to finish the duvet cover.

You Will Need

Duvet

Fabric, in the desired color and pattern

Flat bedsheet

Buttons, in color and style to complement fabric

Scissors, straight pins, tape measure, sewing machine, matching thread

1 Measure the duvet. Purchase or seam together fabric to these dimensions, adding 1 inch to each dimension for seam allowances and keeping in mind that you may require extra yardage for pattern matching (Photo A).

2 Cut or stitch the bedsheet to match the dimensions of the fabric. Finish the top edge of the fabric and bedsheet with a ½-inch hem.

3 Place the fabric and bedsheet right sides together; pin (Photo B). Stitch around the two sides and bottom with a ½-inch seam allowance, leaving the top edge open. Turn right side out.

4 Evenly space buttonholes along the top edge of the fabric. Stitch the buttons to the bedsheet backing to correspond with the buttonholes.

5 Stuff the duvet into the duvet cover and button the cover closed.

A

B

FURNITURE (101)

Most often, the big dollar investment in a room is the furniture. To avoid replacement costs, choose pieces that will fit in well with the desired style, stand up to everyday use, and fit the scale of the room. That's hard enough to do when you're furnishing an empty room; when you're redoing a room, it can be a major hurdle. Here are a few smart ideas for getting

A

good furniture inexpensively and making your existing furniture work better in your rooms.

Thrift Store Finds

Due to the sheer volume and varying condition of the pieces, it takes a good eye to spot the right piece in a thrift store. Before you go, have the measurements of the piece you're looking for and a clear picture in your mind of the elements (such as style and shape) the right piece must have. Thrift store inventory is always changing, so when you're planning to redo a room, make a habit of stopping in often to check what's available. Because these pieces have already been used, check an item carefully before buying it. Sit on chairs to see whether the seat is level, the joints are solid, and the height is right. In fact, checking the joints on every piece is a good idea. If a table or chair is wobbly, or a dresser is

Ⓐ Only sealer was applied to these unfinished dressers, so the warm natural tone of the wood shows through. See page 110 for this room.

out of square, you'll have some work to do to get it back in shape, and you'll have to decide if it's worth the time and expense to do so.

Unfinished Options

Unfinished furniture is another cost-effective option. Although you'll be putting on the finish, it's new furniture and should be good quality. Some pieces require assembly, so you may need clamps and other tools.

Nonetheless, the great thing about unfinished pieces is that you can stain or paint them in any manner to coordinate with other pieces you already have. If you've never put a finish on furniture before, carefully select materials for the job and read the manufacturer's instructions prior to beginning. Varnishes and paints emit fumes, so work in a well-ventilated place.

Hardware

Sprucing up an existing furnishing, such as an everyday dresser, can be as easy as updating the hardware. Changing exposed hinges and drawer pulls—available in nearly every shape,

B The round shape, dark wood tone, and heavy base of this thrift store table make it a perfect match for the Moroccan style of this room. See page 80 for this room.

size, finish, and motif imaginable—is a great way to create a new look on an old piece. If you don't plan to refinish the piece, choose new hardware that's the same size or larger than the old pieces; otherwise, the outline from the old hardware will be exposed.

Fabric

Upholstered pieces are surprisingly versatile and effective when a change of style is desired. Reupholstering or slipcovering can give an old sofa or chair new life. Do-it-yourselfers can reupholster a chair seat, a footstool, or a plain headboard; however, more-complicated proj-

ects require tools and materials that only a professional reupholsterer would have. Although reupholstering a piece may be as expensive as buying new furniture, it's worthwhile if you're getting the piece you really want.

Slipcovers can quickly change the look of a chair or sofa. Slipcovering sofas can be a complicated job, but ready-made slipcovers in all sizes and colors are available; adding trims can give a ready-made slipcover a custom look.

C A graceful lavender slipcover with pleated corners turn this bench into an attractive feature at the end of the bed. See page 110 for this room.

A

BEFORE

A KITCHEN, BOLD (AND) BRIGHT

Galley-style kitchens—long, narrow spaces built between two parallel walls—are often very efficient because the sink and appliances are within easy reach of one another. However, cabinet and countertop space may be limited. This kitchen suffered from a lack of work surfaces and storage space; after its *Design on a Dime* makeover, the room is clutter-free and wears a brand-new look.

Design Team

Kristan Cunningham, Spencer Anderson, Dave Sheinkopf

The Situation

• Cabinet and countertop space is limited. Necessary cooking supplies and utensils sit out in the open.

• The kitchen has an established color scheme—white and bright green—that lends itself to a European bistro feel. However, it lacks accessories and accents that would complete the look.

• The breakfast nook furnishings are uninspired.

• Three small rugs clutter the minimal floor space.

The Solutions

• To reduce clutter a custom pot rack is added above the stove, freeing up valuable countertop and cabinet space.

• With the white and green scheme as a starting point, bright candy colors are added on the walls, windows, and floor.

• The breakfast nook table gets fresh linens and is framed by a clever window treatment.

• A large floorcloth painted with bright fruit motifs covers the entire length of the cooking area; the floorcloth is nonskid and easy to clean.

A Kitchen That Hums with Efficiency

When you want a fresh new look and the budget is minimal, consider what you already have and how it can be retained for the newly decorated space. Kitchens can be a makeover challenge because new cabinets, countertops, and appliances are big investments. Fortunately, this homeowner had already made some smart moves before the *Design on a Dime* team arrived on the scene: The old cabinets were spiffed up with a coat of white paint and the doors became accents in a zippy green. The existing white appliances blend perfectly with the light-color space (dark appliances would stand out against the light-color walls, cabinets, and floors, making the space appear even smaller).

To make this kitchen function well, the first thing to address

Ⓐ Punched-up colors turn a drab narrow space into a pleasant sunny spot. Ⓑ Hanging pots and utensils above the stove puts a tiny alcove to use and frees up cupboard space. Ⓒ Pert patterns and spicy colors come together well when the patterns are all geometrics and black and white act as anchor colors.

was storage. In any kitchen, it is important to have ample countertop space for food preparation. To free up counter space, a pot rack fashioned from a curved piece of hefty hammered metal is hung above the stove, where it stays out of the way and keeps pots, pans, and utensils within easy reach. This makes great use of space that was previously used only for a decorative trivet.

Kitchens also require adequate light to work by. This kitchen had two bare-bulb fixtures, hung on opposite ends of the room. Although these provided enough light for the small space, they weren't attractive. Now, two pendants made of brushed silver, a large outer glass globe, and a small frosted-yellow globe add pizzazz to the room. On the floor, three rag rugs dotted the bland vinyl tile. In their place now resides a large floorcloth, painted with colorful fruit motifs. The floorcloth provides a nonskid surface that's perfect for a kitchen and adds a much-needed dose of color to the floor.

Focus on Dining

Many galley kitchens lack a designated dining space. Here, however, a small green metal table and two chairs positioned in a small sliver of space provide a great place to read the paper or converse with the cook. The

A pot rack fashioned from a curved piece of metal is hung above the stove, where it stays out of the way and keeps pots, pans, and utensils within easy reach.

Floorcloths

Floorcloths made of preprimed canvas are an inexpensive, easy way to add style, color, and pattern to any room. Preprimed canvas—canvas treated with artist's gesso—is available in many shapes and sizes at crafts and art supply stores and from online vendors. Most canvas is nonfraying, so it can be cut with scissors or a rotary cutter into any desired shape, such as squares, rectangles, ovals, and circles. Some older types of canvas may require hemming with an adhesive, such as hot glue. Readily available acrylic paints were used to paint this floorcloth with vivid oversize fruit motifs and a wavy border. Because of its large size, this canvas was stretched on an easel; however, floorcloths can also be created on a tabletop covered with plastic or newsprint. To protect the canvas against wear and to make it washable, the top is treated to two coats of clear acrylic polyurethane. Floorcloths are nonslip by nature. For added security, attach a nonskid backing.

table and chairs have the right size and scale for this space and create a casual atmosphere in the room. Because the outdoor furnishings seem stark and bare in the space, fabric is used to draw them into the space. A checked tablecloth—in a golden color that nearly matches the new gold wall paint—covers the table; tufted cushions in a dotted motif pad the chair seats. Black and white checkerboard napkins provide accents. This bold blend of color and pattern dresses up the furnishings and contributes to a European bistro feel.

The window above the eating nook receives a treatment that covers only the bottom portion. This treatment, which replaces unattractive miniblinds, features a warm solid-color red fabric and a gold and red striped fabric. It lets in light while providing privacy.

A A floorcloth with an oversize pattern visually grounds the room. The large size of the floorcloth itself has greater impact than the small throw rugs could provide. **B** Sleek lighting adds style without drawing too much attention upward.

Floorcloths are inexpensive; I can choose any size or shape that I want, and I can choose any color and design for the room. —Dave Sheinkopf

Restyle with Lively Fabrics and Accessories

Eye-popping color—sunny yellow, spicy red, cool springlike green, and dashes of black thrown in as an accent—transforms this kitchen from blah to brilliant. A yellow-orange on the walls—created by mixing paint with transparent glaze and applying the mixture with a soft lint-free rag—is a subtle background treatment that keeps the focus on the brighter cabinets. The yellow-orange also creates a backdrop for the red window treatments and the black accents, including the colorful framed prints above the table and the dark metal pot rack. The use of glaze creates depth and dimension on the formerly bland white walls.

The mix of patterns, such as the wavy inner border on the floorcloth and the various dotted and checked fabrics, present throughout the space keeps things interesting. Because the same colors—red and yellow—are repeated in the fabrics, all the fabrics mix and blend well. The black and white checked fabric is the largest pattern of those used in the room; its large size anchors the other various-size fabric patterns.

A Covering only the lower half of the window provides privacy while letting in the sunshine. Combining two fabrics gives the small curtains lots of decorator impact. **B** Outdoor furniture fit the nook well but offered little visual or physical comfort. Thick chair pads and a long tablecloth solved both problems.

POT RACK

Making your own pot rack is easy and economical. If you are unable to find a piece of metal—curved or straight—that you like at a home improvement store, check industrial metal shops for a wide range of styles, from clean-lined modern pieces to elaborate decorative designs. Spencer purchased the metal for this project at a machining shop, which also shaped the piece to prepare it for its new life as a pot rack. The piece used is a dark hammered metal that's perfect to achieve the old-world European look in this kitchen.

Now this is what I've been looking for. It screams Euro bistro, and it's going to make an awesome pot rack. And, for only $20, it's well within our budget.
—Spencer Anderson, while shopping for metal

You Will Need

Piece of metal in desired shape and size
Drill, heavy-duty metal drill bit
2 plant hooks, 2 lengths of chain
S hooks
Tape measure

1 Determine how many utensils you would like to hang from the rack; drill this number of evenly spaced holes along the bottom edge of the metal piece.

2 Drill two holes in the top of the metal piece, about 6 inches from each end (Photo A); attach the two pieces of chain through the holes.

3 Insert the plant hooks into the ceiling, spacing them about as far apart as the chains. Hang the rack (Photo B).

4 Insert the S hooks into the holes at the bottom of the rack.

A

B

BEFORE

FIT FOR (A) FAMILY

This family room is the center of the house: It is used for everything from relaxing to doing homework. Although most of the components are in place for a well-functioning, good-looking room, the space lacks cohesive style. The *Design on a Dime* team uses smart arranging approaches, takes advantage of underutilized space, and plays up the furnishings and accessories the homeowner already has. Follow these cues to create a family-friendly haven of your own.

Design Team

Kristan Cunningham, Spencer Anderson, Dave Sheinkopf

The Situation

• Although this large room has plenty of space for family activity furnishings, the layout doesn't allow for the best visiting or TV viewing.

• The nook beneath the stairs is used for open storage/display space; although it's an asset, it isn't used to its full potential.

• Storage is a problem: Paper and books are in full view beneath the coffee table and sofa table, and the TV and electronic components are in open view on a small entertainment center.

• The room lacks a defined style.

The Solutions

• Repositioning the sofa and love seat to face each other takes advantage of the space, and the arrangement better suits the activities that take place here.

• The existing chair and table lamp are moved to the nook; with the addition of a small side table, the nook becomes an inviting spot for reading.

• To corral clutter, the TV and equipment go in an armoire; storage ottomans are also added.

• Existing pieces and new items are combined for a comfortable yet contemporary room.

Arranged for Living

Although large rooms offer ample space for multiple furnishings, the space is often underused. In this living room a large sofa, a love seat, and a chair are crowded in a corner, leaving empty floor space. Positioned nearly in front of a large window, the TV occupies a small stand crowded with electronics and books. A small side table is tucked in the corner of the L created by the sofas. A coffee table and a sofa table, prone to clutter, complete the grouping.

To make this space more usable, the major furnishings are repositioned: The sofa is moved closer to the corner, and the love seat is shifted to face the sofa; the TV, housed in a new armoire, takes the spot where the love seat used to be. Now family members and guests can easily converse or watch TV, and the new location away from the

(A) Moving the sofa and love seat opposite each other makes both conversation and TV watching easier. (B) A small armoire houses the television and electronics and hides them when they're not in use. (C) A clean-lined coffee table made from plywood and purchased square legs matches the contemporary style of the armoire.

Living Room Storage Solutions

Because living rooms are natural gathering places for families, stuff tends to accumulate there. Charles Burbridge offers these terrific ideas for controlling clutter in your living room:

Organization is key! Rooms often have multiple functions; the living room becomes the living/dining/family/study/office/project room. With all those uses comes clutter, and with clutter comes sprawl. So many storage problems can be eliminated by getting organized. My motto: A place for everything and everything in its place.

Lidded containers are a utilitarian yet attractive way of containing clutter. An interesting wooden box or woven basket is a great improvement over that convenient (yet totally unattractive) pile of magazines you've created next to the sofa. When you add good lidded containers to your room, cleanup is as easy as putting the lids back on!

Double-duty furniture pieces maximize limited storage options. For instance, an armoire with a few interior shelves can house your entire home entertainment system with room to spare. An ottoman or bench seat can double as a coffee table with storage hidden within.

window also protects TV viewers from glaring sunlight. To conceal clutter and eliminate distractions, the armoire doors can be closed when the TV is not in use.

New custom tables, in better scale with existing furnishings, replace the coffee table and sofa table. The tables are built from 4×8 sheets

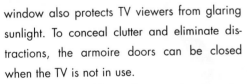

A A favorite chair gets its own spot in a designated reading corner under the stairs. B Family photos taken by the homeowner become inexpensive art when placed in standard-size purchased mats and frames. C Plywood and purchased legs create a quick console table. The rich wood tones of the tabletop match the homeowner's string bass, which has been brought out of storage.

of 1¼-inch birch plywood; the edges of the medium-tone pieces have walnut veneer tape, and the tops are protected with semigloss polyurethane—a must for furniture that will receive everyday wear and require cleaning. The coffee table is finished with square parsons legs and the sofa table has slim aluminum legs.

To bring warmth to the wide-open room, the walls are painted a soft green-beige. The subdued color allows the furnishings—the darker green sofas and medium-tone armoire and tables—to take center stage.

To bring the look together, lighting and windows are addressed. The large window, formerly

BEFORE

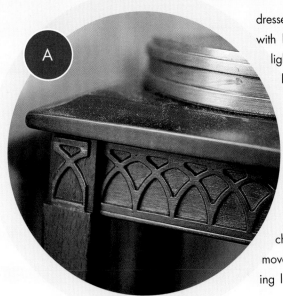

dressed in vinyl vertical blinds, now is covered with light-tone bamboo shades. For privacy or light control, dark blue panels hung from a light-tone wood rod can be drawn closed. To complete the lighting, two tall floor lamps with paper shades flank the armoire.

A Nice Nook

The niche under the stairs held knick-knacks on a bookshelf and a string bass. To take advantage of the area, a favorite chair—in muted green, blue, and cream—is moved in along with a new side table and existing lamp. The shapely motifs in the side table

table and sofa table. In addition, the ottomans can be used for seating.

Accessorize with What You Love

Previously, this room was void of artwork or decorative elements. All it took to complete the look was an evaluation of what the homeowner had already.

First, the homeowner, an amateur photographer, had family photographs ready to be called into action. With ready-cut mats and black frames, the prints flanking the armoire are given importance. Above the sofa, two additional prints get wide mats and narrow silver

Shelving is a fantastic way to get rid of tabletop clutter and give back a usable surface. Shelves also represent a great display opportunity. —Charles Burbridge

mimic the curved lamp base. Pewter polish wiped on the bright brass tones it down. The new lampshade, more in scale with the base, has black grosgrain ribbon embellishment. This nook is now a haven rather than an eyesore.

Next to the nook, new storage ottomans keep toys and paperwork within easy reach. The ottomans are constructed from medium-density fiberboard (MDF), painted, then covered with batting and fabric. Casters add mobility. These new storage pieces collect the clutter that formerly accumulated beneath the coffee

frames. Matting and framing is an easy, inexpensive way to decorate.

Next, the homeowner's string bass is brought out from its case, adding a sophisticated unfussy touch.

Finally, new elements enliven the space: light-tone baskets on the coffee table and armoire, colorful apples on the coffee table, and a tree near the armoire.

A The carved designs on the end table blend with the motifs on the reading chair and lamp. Grouping all the shapely pieces in one area makes them look planned, not plunked. **B** Bamboo shades keep the window light and bright. Darker fabric panels can be closed when more privacy is needed.

STORAGE OTTOMAN

Add extra storage—for little expense—with a pair of upholstered cubes. Spencer Anderson created these examples from medium-density fiberboard (MDF) for only $53! The fabric and padding softens the look and makes the cubes appropriate for extra seating. Casters on the bottom make them easy to move.

One of the problems we need to address in this living room is the lack of storage space. Because the homeowner and his kids spend a lot of time there, I thought it would be nice to give them some extra seating, so I made these two ottomans.
—Spencer Anderson

You Will Need

Medium-density fiberboard (MDF)
Wood glue
Drill, assorted bits
1-inch drywall screws
Sandpaper
Paint to coordinate with fabric, paintbrush
Piano hinges, screws
Staple gun, staples
Fabric, quilt batting
Hot-glue gun, glue sticks
Ribbon to match the fabric
4 flat-base caster wheels, appropriate screws

1 Determine the size and dimension for the cubes. Because butt joints are used, two sides are shorter by the thickness of the MDF times two. Cut the sides, top, and bottom of the cube.

2 Join the four side pieces with butt joints using wood glue and 1-inch drywall screws. Attach the bottom piece. Lightly sand all the pieces. Paint the cube and the top.

3 Wrap the cube with batting, extending the batting 1 inch over the inside and underside of the cube. Staple and glue the batting in place. Cut the batting to fit the top and tack it in place with hot glue.

4 Cut fabric 1 inch longer and 2 inches wider than the cube. Cut fabric for the lid 1 inch larger all around. Starting at one back corner, staple the fabric over the batting. Wrap the fabric around the cube to the beginning, turn under the raw edges, and staple it in place. Wrap fabric around the top and staple it in place. Conceal the edges with ribbon.

5 Attach the top to the cube with piano hinges.

6 Attach caster wheels to the bottom.

A

BEFORE

COOL COLLEGE STYLE (FOR) TWO

Life in a dorm room has its ups and downs—and the downs often involve sharing tight quarters with another person. Trying to cram everything two people need, including clothes, books, and personal treasures, into a small space can be problematic. In this 12x14 room, shared by two young men, the *Design on a Dime* team used innovative solutions to create a stylish retreat that's perfect for studying, sleeping, and playing.

Design Team

Lee Snijders, Summer Baltzer, Charles Burbridge

The Situation

• This small space is shared by two college-age young men; the current layout doesn't allow for any activity to be done comfortably.

• Storage space is insufficient for all the stuff college students accumulate.

• Light comes from two small desk lamps, a ceiling fixture, and one window.

• The walls are home to a smattering of posters, photographs, and school mementos; a more organized, attractive arrangement is needed.

The Solutions

• The beds are raised off the floor on loft frames; the desks are positioned at the end of each loft, and new comfortable chairs and bookcases are added beneath each bed as a place to relax.

• In order to keep clutter at a minimum, additional bookcases are added, and a new large rolling storage unit is constructed.

• To meet the lighting needs, a combination of clip lights, new desk lamps, and wall-mounted fixtures are brought into the room.

• Magnetic boards linked by chains hang from the wall and display cherished photographs.

Room for Sleep

When space is limited, it's important to find solutions that open up floor space. Originally, the low beds were positioned in an L shape, with a desk situated in the corner of the L (a very cramped study space). To conserve space and clean up the untidy open storage under the beds, loft frames are created to raise the beds off the floor; the space beneath accommodates new matching chairs, ottomans, and bookcases, which together make a cozy spot for reading and relaxing. The new configuration even leaves room for additional storage pieces to be added, an important consideration in a small space shared by two people.

High on the wall above each bed, a shelf is added to act as a nightstand, a great place to stash books and favorite photographs. Also, task lights are

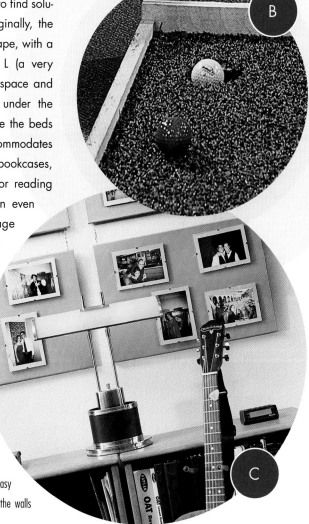

A The whole room gets a lift when the beds are raised to create seating underneath. **B** To aid in relaxation—and golfing skills—a two-part putting green is created. **C** Magnetic picture boards make it easy to display (and change) photographs while keeping the walls clutter-free.

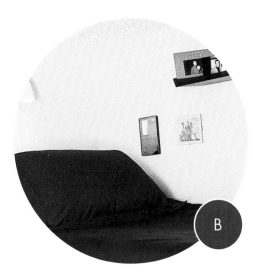

Storage On the Go

Charles Burbridge called this room "spacially challenged." To help create a space that can handle the belongings of two, he made this tall shelving unit—that doesn't take up much floor space—for $75. The unit, created from hardboard, has open shelves on both sides, so each student can easily get what he needs. There's also a corkboard that's a great place to tack up notes and photographs. The unit is set on wheels so that it can be moved around the room to accommodate different furniture arrangements.

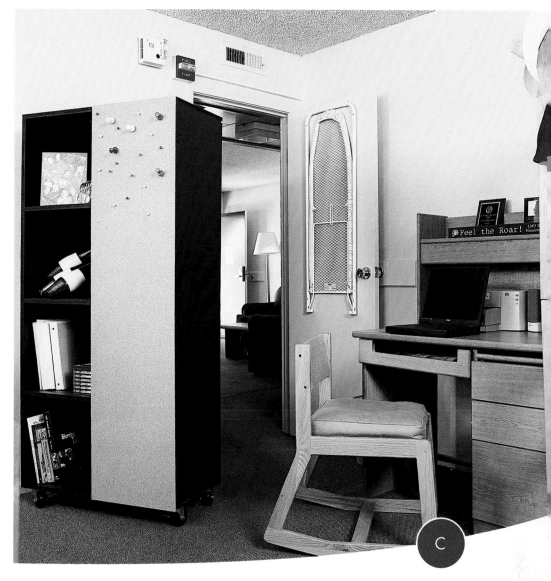

attached to the wall above the head of each bed, providing crucial light for late-night reading. Finally, the mismatched bedding is removed, and new solid-color comforters are added. To avoid an overly coordinated look, two comforter colors are used—navy blue and burgundy, the school's colors. These colors also define each student's study binders.

Room for Study

Previously, the desks were positioned against two walls—one in the corner of the L formed by the beds, the other in front of the large window.

The desks and chairs (with the old bed pillows used as cushions) are now moved to the end of each loft, within arm's reach of the movable storage unit. Positioning the desks under the lofts may not have allowed for sufficient light for studying, even with the addition of new desk lamps. However, the comfortable chairs and

---

Ⓐ With the beds raised off the floor, space opens up below for a chair and bookcases. Ⓑ A narrow shelf takes the place of a nightstand for each loft bed, letting the residents display personal items and store bedside necessities, such as lighting and a clock. Ⓒ Additional storage doubles as a room divider when the cabinet is placed on wheels.

ottomans under the beds can be used for studying as well as relaxing.

Throughout the room new lighting fixtures are added to ensure adequate illumination for various activities. New lamps appear on each desk, floor lamps are placed beside each new chair, and a stylish lamp stands on the existing bookcases, offering a lot more options than the original ceiling fixture and desk lamps.

Room for Storage

Storage is almost always a problem in small spaces, and the problem is compounded when the space is shared by two people and all their

need arises, for instance to create a private area (if positioned behind one desk).

Room for Fun

Fun is an essential part of college! Originally, this room didn't have any space for relaxing, hanging out with friends, or even enjoying favorite pastimes.

To make this room fun as well as functional, space had to be made for personal expression. A grid of magnetic boards is created, on which clip photo frames are arranged. Hung on the far wall above the twin bookcases, the boards are an instant focal point. Additional photographs of fun, family, and friends are displayed on the desks and shelf nightstands.

To make a small space appear larger, make use of wall space for storage. It always cleans up a room when you take the stuff off the floor and put it on the walls. —Spencer Anderson

belongings, including books, binders, and clothing. Previously, the only storage spaces available were two small bookcases and plastic bins stacked beneath the beds. Both the bookcases and bins were cramped, and both were in plain view from the entrance of the room.

The existing bookcases remain, repositioned at the far end of the wall, within easy reach of the desks and chairs. Larger metal bookcases are added beneath each loft, and stylish metal storage boxes are placed on the shelves to contain small items and note cards. Finally, a tall movable storage unit is built to provide additional concealed storage space. Constructed of ¾-inch hardboard, the unit is partially covered with corkboard, which is a great place to tack messages and photographs. The wheels allow the storage unit to be moved around when the

One of the students is a guitarist; he needed space to play. The guitar now has a prominent space in the room, showcased beneath the grid photo display. The other student enjoys golfing; to encourage his hobby, a collapsible putting green made of a plywood frame and synthetic turf is built (the two pieces make removal and storage easy). This innovative piece now provides an ideal study break—and a great way to practice.

A Desks move to the ends of the beds where there is plenty of room and light. The bookcases under the lofts and at the end of the room allow the desks to remain clear and useable.

Know the Rules

The *Design on a Dime* team faced quite a challenge in this college dorm room. It had to abide by dorm rules: no removing of the window treatments and ceiling light fixture, and no damaging the walls with nails. Such things are important to know, whether you are a student in a dorm or an apartment renter; before you begin to redecorate, read your lease carefully to ensure you don't do anything you'll need to repair or pay for later.

MAGNETIC PICTURE BOARD

Most students like to display photographs of family and friends, new and old. Taping them directly to the wall is easy and inexpensive but not at all stylish. The *Design on a Dime* team offers this creative solution: four magnetic boards linked together, on which photographs are clipped. The photos can easily be changed when the desire arises, and only four holes are drilled into the wall for hanging.

Summer has figured out a way to display pictures that will cause minimal damage to the dorm room walls.

—*Lee Snijders on Summer's magnetic picture boards*

You Will Need

4 sheets of 18x20" magnetic board
4 decorative hooks
Thin-gauge chain, wire
Magnets
5x6" lightweight picture holders
Hot-glue gun, glue sticks
Drill, titanium drill bit
Wire snips

1 Drill four holes into the top and bottom frames of two magnetic boards (for a total of eight holes in each) as the upper boards; for the remaining two (lower) boards, drill four holes in the top only.

2 Arrange the four boards in a grid pattern. Using the wire, connect the four boards with short (approximately 4-inch) lengths of chain, threading the wire through the chain ends and through the holes in the boards (Photo A). Attach lengths of chain to the top of the two upper boards for hanging.

3 Drill four holes in the wall, corresponding with the location of the holes in the tops of the two upper boards.

4 Attach the hooks to the wall; hang the linked boards from the hooks (Photo B).

5 Glue magnets to the back of the picture holders (Photo C). Attach the picture holders to the boards as desired.

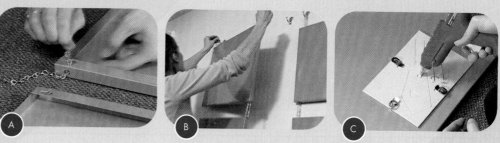

For a video demonstration of this project and more
Design on a Dime ideas, visit HGTV.com/dod

A

BEFORE

A GETAWAY FOR GUESTS

Whether used often or once a year, guest rooms need to be relaxing places where guests can retire for a peaceful night's sleep. This uninspired space with white walls was a holding tank for mismatched pieces—an oversize sofa and filing cabinets that were out of place in the small bedroom. If you desire a stylish guest room, take some lessons from this makeover. Who knows? You may love your new guest room so much that you make it your own getaway!

Design Team

Kristan Cunningham, Spencer Anderson, Dave Sheinkopf

The Situation

• This guest room is home to mismatched furnishings, including a large sofa and filing cabinets, that are unsuitable for the space.

• The bed is an air mattress, on a low frame. Without a headboard and with its dated bedding, the bed lacks status and appeal.

• The small room has no color or defined style.

The Solutions

• The oversize sofa and filing cabinets are removed, making way for a more streamlined table and chair and floating nightstands (slim wall-mounted shelves).

• A new frame and mattress are brought into the room. A new handmade headboard and sophisticated bedding give the bed a stronger presence and a lot more appeal.

• With the addition of brown and green paint—and a bold red circle for contrast—the walls become artwork. A thin band of molding, a sophisticated window treatment over a rice paper shade, and sleek accessories add interesting detail to the space.

A Commanding Presence

This room previously housed an air mattress on a low frame. Although it functioned, it wasn't the most comfortable option, and it certainly wasn't an inspired focal point: With no headboard, the bed floated against a sea of white walls, and the old-fashion country quilt and single pillow were unattractive. To give the bed a more commanding presence in the room—and add grown-up appeal—a proper frame and mattress are added; then a large-scale headboard is constructed, and luxurious silk bedding finishes the look.

The headboard is created from plywood and pillow forms; the rich chocolate brown fabric appears tufted, thanks to a grid of metal strips and nailhead tacks. Small brushed-silver lamps are clipped to either side of the headboard unit, providing light for late-night reading.

Ⓐ The contemporary look centers on a headboard made from fabric-padded plywood and narrow strips of aluminum. Ⓑ A stylish chair and side table provide seating and a small work space. Ⓒ A slim shelf has minimal display space yet lots of interest, especially when set off-center on a painted circle.

To create a welcoming spot for guests, the bed is treated to a quilted silk comforter in a cool green that complements the upper portion of the walls. A tailored bed skirt in beige, crisp white sheets and pillowcases, and two small decorative pillows in a contemporary green and beige motif join the comforter for grown-up appeal.

Two slim shelves that act as nightstands are attached to the walls; they replace the filing cabinets that previously served this purpose. These shelves save precious floor space and allow enough room for guest bedroom essentials, such as a clock, reading materials, and a candle for ambiance.

the bottom strip of metal in the headboard and the fabric band in the window treatment.

To further establish the bed as the focal point—and to add some flair to the floor—a highly textured sisal rug with a chocolate brown band is positioned at the foot of the bed. This earthy touch complements the newly established color palette; the texture of the rug contrasts with the silk bedding and industrial-style furnishings.

High-Class Touches on a Budget

To keep this room sleek and contemporary, minimal furnishings and embellishments are added.

First, the window treatments are addressed. Previously, the window was dressed in a frilly cream-color valance and matching panels, with

This room is lacking a major focal point, so I thought the perfect solution was to make a customized headboard. —Spencer Anderson

Earthy Colors and Textures Ground the Room

A combination of chocolate brown, green, and beige gives this room contemporary flair. All the colors come together on the focal-point bed; the brown and two shades of green unite for a unique color scheme on the walls. Deep olive green resides on the lower third of the walls, firmly grounding the design, and bright green inhabits the upper two-thirds. Using the lighter, brighter color on the upper portion makes the room appear larger; the lighter color soars toward the ceiling and opens up the room.

The two colors are separated by a narrow band of molding that flows around the entire room. The molding, painted in a dark chocolate brown, also helps to visually ground the room: All the furnishings rest below the band, which aligns perfectly with

(A) Kristan creates the circle on the wall with the help of a large compass with chalk on one end.

ordinary blinds underneath. To take the style up a notch, the blinds are replaced by a more attractive rice paper shade. Then, a single fabric panel is created; it repeats the wall color in exact alignment, right down to a narrow strip of fabric that mimics the molding. This smart use of fabric gives a sense of continuity throughout the space; when the curtains are closed, occupants feel enveloped in a streamlined setting.

Next, to provide seating space, a sleek chair and table are added, replacing the oversize sofa. Both table and chair are made of metal, complementing the metal-accent headboard. A slim lamp stands on the table, providing a touch of ambient light and eliminating the need for the unattractive halogen lamp.

The final detail is a slender wall shelf, positioned on a painted circle opposite the bed. Because the headboard has such a commanding presence, and the walls themselves act as artwork, minimal decorating is required; the painted circle and shelf are enough.

PADDED HEADBOARD

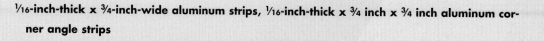

Set yourself up for comfort with a padded headboard that is mounted directly to the wall. A grid created by metal strips gives the headboard a clean, contemporary look and also keeps the pillows from shifting.

B After the headboard is complete, Spencer and Dave mount it to the wall above the bed for a one-of-a-kind focal point.

Project Pointers

The use of a scarf joint—where two pieces of MDF are cut at an angle so that they lock together—makes this headboard easy to hang. To take strain off the scarf joint, you can attach a strip of MDF to the back of the headboard, near the bottom, that is the same depth as the joint. This keeps the headboard a uniform distance from the wall (so that it doesn't have a tendency to tip).

You Will Need

Medium-density fiberboard (MDF), circular saw

Tape measure

¾-inch drywall screws, stud finder

Square pillow forms

Fabric, scissors, staple gun, staples

Aviation snips or tin snips

Carriage bolts, nuts

Drill, bits, flathead screws

1/16-inch-thick x ¾-inch-wide aluminum strips, 1/16-inch-thick x ¾ inch x ¾ inch aluminum corner angle strips

1 Cut the MDF to the width of the bed and the desired height. Lay the pillow forms on the MDF in the desired pattern (Photo A). Staple the edges of the pillows to the MDF (Photo B). Stretch the fabric over the pillows; staple the fabric to the back of the MDF.

2 Cut the aluminum strips to the lengths needed to cover the joins of the pillows. Attach the strips to the MDF using carriage bolts, tufting the pillows; secure the bolts on the back with nuts. Attach the aluminum corner angle strips to the edges of the MDF using flathead screws (Photo C).

3 Cut a piece of MDF the width of the headboard and 12 inches high. Rip the MDF in half width-wise at a 50-degree angle to create a scarf joint. Attach one piece to the wall using drywall screws and the stud finder, where the center of the headboard will hang. Attach the remaining piece to the back of the headboard. Secure the headboard to the wall by "locking" the MDF pieces together.

A

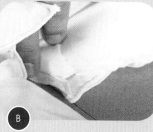

B

C

WINDOW TREATMENTS ⑩①

Window treatments are both a functional and an aesthetic addition to any room: They let in light, provide privacy, and contribute color to a space. When choosing what type of treatment you want for a particular room, consider what you see when looking out a window, and what someone could see looking in. Also consider how many windows are in the room:

A The ready-made tab-top panels in this dining area are customized with bands of colorful striped fabric. See page 86 for this room.

several windows of the same size grouped together, for example, or a couple of windows of different sizes on opposite walls. Then evaluate how much light and air the window provides and how much of that you want to preserve. Glaring sunlight and fume-filled breezes from the street are two reasons for installing heartier window coverings. Together, these key elements will help you choose the right window treatment for your needs.

Beyond the practical considerations, you have style choices to make too. A valance, cornice, or swag can top your treatment; to frame the edges you can use curtains or draperies, which come in many varieties, from tab-top to those with a rod pocket. And, shades and blinds can be spruced up with a coat of paint or bands of ribbon or fabric.

The choices for window treatments are limit-

less. Here are some additional things to consider when selecting the right treatments for your particular room and needs:

• If the view isn't great or the light is overly harsh, minimize the visual importance of a window by covering it with a shade or shutters. Both choices allow you to adjust the amount of light coming in. Consider the shades in the living room *opposite bottom right* (and on pages 62 to 69). They block glare while still allowing light in, and their texture adds visual interest. The shaded window recedes, becoming a backdrop for a chest that displays a pleasant grouping of accessories.

• Windows let in sound and heat or cold as well as light and views. Lined curtains or drapes can mitigate those elements. Look at the nursery on pages 92 to 99. The bank of windows lets in plenty of light and fresh air. When the baby is sleeping, the lined shades can be drawn to block the light and muffle noise. The neat stripes are accented with a row of pom-pom trim at the bottom, a small detail that adds flair.

• Treatments can reshape a window. To make

B King-size bedsheets are embellished with a luxurious quilted fabric to enhance the sophisticated feel in this bedroom. See page 146 for this room.

a small window look larger, hang draperies several inches above and outside the window frame, and let them hang to the floor. The actual shape of the wide awning window that sits high on the wall is much less obvious because of how the draperies are hung in the bedroom *above* (and on pages 146 to 151). The shirred top and a panel along the bottom are made of a quilted fabric, a sophisticated accent to the white center panels, which were created from king-size bedsheets. White shades cover the window and blend into the wall when drawn, making the window almost unnoticeable.

• Consider all the windows in a room when selecting a treatment. Not all the window coverings need to match, but if they're coordinated, the room gains a cohesive look. The two-tone tab-top curtains on the French doors in the dining area *opposite* (and on pages 86 to 91) are repeated in a shorter version on a side window. If you can't find a perfectly matching selection in packaged window treatments, start with a standard curtain, like this tab-top, and add a complementary fabric to the bottom.

C Rice paper shades let in light and also provide privacy. The texture of the shades complements the Asian decor in this living room. See page 62 for this room.

ROOM ARRANGING KIT

Now that you've seen all the great tips and tricks the *Design on a Dime* hosts and design coordinators use to create inviting, flexible rooms, it's time to design a room that fits your needs and lifestyle. This section includes easy-to-use furniture templates and a grid so that you can plot the arrangement of your room just like the pros—using your existing furnishings or those you plan to purchase.

How to Use This Kit

• Measure the room, then plot the dimensions on the grid provided or graph paper with one square equaling one square foot.

• Draw windows with a double line and leave an open space for doorways. Use the architectural symbols to draw such elements as bifold doors and fireplaces.

• Measure each piece of furniture to be placed in the room. Trace or photocopy the corresponding templates, then cut them out with scissors or a crafts knife. Note that some of the templates, such as the sofas and beds, are shown in multiple sizes, but feel free to create templates of special sizes or for unique furnishings.

• Using the cut templates, experiment with different configurations and build around established focal points, such as a fireplace, or create them with large-scale furnishings, accessories, or artwork.

Ⓐ Due to its positioning beneath a high window and the inviting bedding, the bed is the undisputed focal point of this room. Ⓑ Lee stacks '50s-style tables in front of a sofa for easy access to beverages.

Room Arrangement Strategies

• To allow for smooth traffic flow around the room there should be at least 3 feet of space around furniture groupings. Also, position the furnishings so that you can easily walk through, in, or out of a room.

• When placing a table in front of a sofa or chairs, keep a minimum of 12 to 18 inches between them; additional space will make it difficult for people who are seated to reach items on the table.

• Side tables should stand about the same height as the arm of the chair or sofa next to it.

• Many furnishings have square edges and legs. Incorporate some round or oval furnishings and accessories to break up the straight lines.

• Create one main focal point in a room to prevent the eye from wandering too much. The exception: Arrange furnishings to take advantage of two focal points that can be viewed at once, such as a fireplace and window with great views.

• Balance is important: Choose furnishings of different heights, shapes, and sizes for interest. The balance will be interrupted if all tall or hefty pieces are placed on one side of the room.

• Keep the size of the room in mind when choosing and positioning furnishings.

UPHOLSTERED FURNITURE AND BEDS

Sofa and Sectional Items

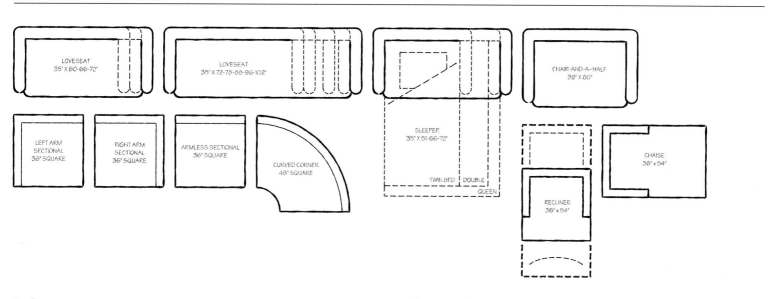

LOVESEAT
35" X 60-66-72"

LOVESEAT
35" X 72-78-88-96-102"

CHAIR-AND-A-HALF
39" X 60"

LEFT ARM
SECTIONAL
36" SQUARE

RIGHT ARM
SECTIONAL
36" SQUARE

ARMLESS SECTIONAL
36" SQUARE

CURVED CORNER
48" SQUARE

SLEEPER
35" X 51-66-72"

TWIN BED | DOUBLE
QUEEN

CHAISE
36" X 54"

RECLINER
36" x 54"

Beds

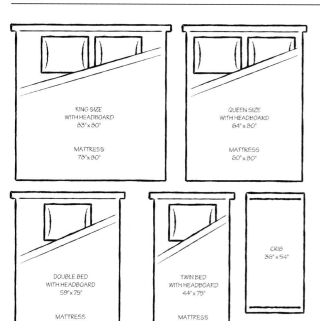

KING SIZE
WITH HEADBOARD
83" X 80"

MATTRESS
78" X 80"

QUEEN SIZE
WITH HEADBOARD
64" X 80"

MATTRESS
60" X 80"

DOUBLE BED
WITH HEADBOARD
59" x 75"

MATTRESS
54" x 75"

TWIN BED
WITH HEADBOARD
44" x 75"

MATTRESS
39" x 75"

CRIB
36" x 54"

Chairs and Ottomans

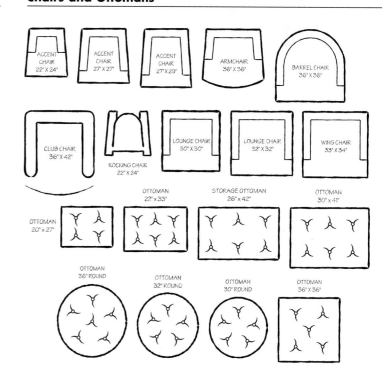

ACCENT
CHAIR
22" X 24"

ACCENT
CHAIR
27" X 27"

ACCENT
CHAIR
27" X 29"

ARMCHAIR
36" X 36"

BARREL CHAIR
36" X 36"

CLUB CHAIR
36" X 42"

ROCKING CHAIR
22" X 24"

LOUNGE CHAIR
30" X 30"

LOUNGE CHAIR
32" X 32"

WING CHAIR
33" X 34"

OTTOMAN
22" X 33"

STORAGE OTTOMAN
26" X 42"

OTTOMAN
30" X 41"

OTTOMAN
20" x 27"

OTTOMAN
36" ROUND

OTTOMAN
32" ROUND

OTTOMAN
30" ROUND

OTTOMAN
36" X 36"

TABLES, OFFICE FURNISHINGS, AND BEYOND

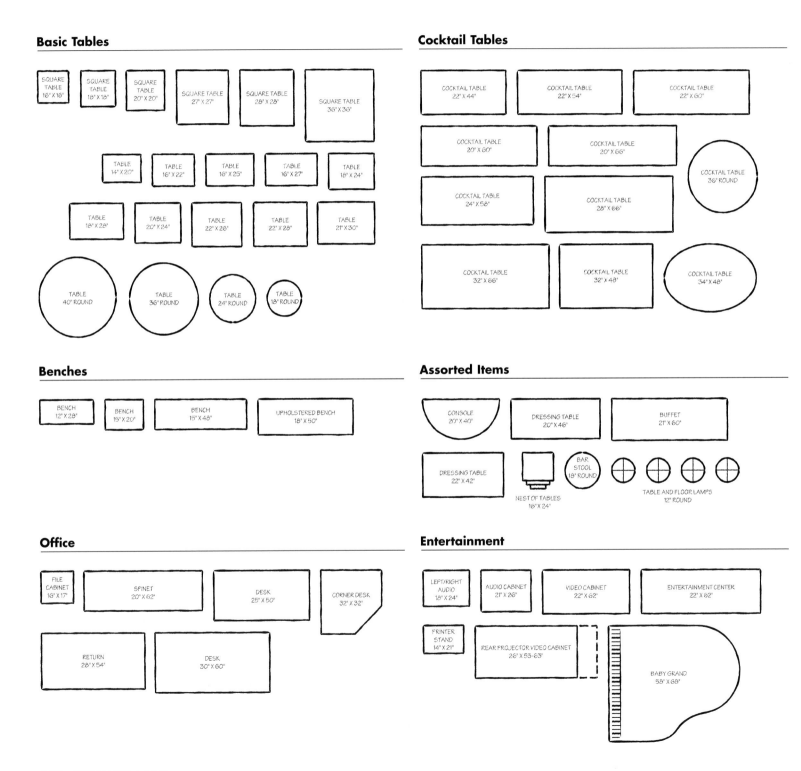

Basic Tables

SQUARE TABLE 16" X 16"

SQUARE TABLE 18" X 18"

SQUARE TABLE 20" X 20"

SQUARE TABLE 27" X 27"

SQUARE TABLE 28" X 28"

SQUARE TABLE 36" X 36"

TABLE 14" X 20"

TABLE 16" X 22"

TABLE 16" X 25"

TABLE 16" X 27"

TABLE 18" X 24"

TABLE 18" X 28"

TABLE 20" X 24"

TABLE 22" X 26"

TABLE 22" X 28"

TABLE 21" X 30"

TABLE 40" ROUND

TABLE 36" ROUND

TABLE 24" ROUND

TABLE 18" ROUND

Cocktail Tables

COCKTAIL TABLE 22" X 44"

COCKTAIL TABLE 22" X 54"

COCKTAIL TABLE 22" X 60"

COCKTAIL TABLE 20" X 60"

COCKTAIL TABLE 20" X 66"

COCKTAIL TABLE 36" ROUND

COCKTAIL TABLE 24" X 58"

COCKTAIL TABLE 28" X 66"

COCKTAIL TABLE 32" X 66"

COCKTAIL TABLE 32" X 48"

COCKTAIL TABLE 34" X 48"

Benches

BENCH 12" X 28"

BENCH 15" X 20"

BENCH 15" X 48"

UPHOLSTERED BENCH 18" X 50"

Assorted Items

CONSOLE 20" X 40"

DRESSING TABLE 20" X 46"

BUFFET 21" X 60"

DRESSING TABLE 22" X 42"

NEST OF TABLES 16" X 24"

BAR STOOL 18" ROUND

TABLE AND FLOOR LAMPS 12" ROUND

Office

FILE CABINET 16" X 17"

SPINET 20" X 62"

DESK 25" X 50"

CORNER DESK 32" X 32"

RETURN 28" X 54"

DESK 30" X 60"

Entertainment

LEFT/RIGHT AUDIO 18" X 24"

AUDIO CABINET 21" X 26"

VIDEO CABINET 22" X 62"

ENTERTAINMENT CENTER 22" X 62"

PRINTER STAND 14" X 21"

REAR PROJECTOR VIDEO CABINET 26" X 53-63"

BABY GRAND 58" X 68"

SYMBOLS

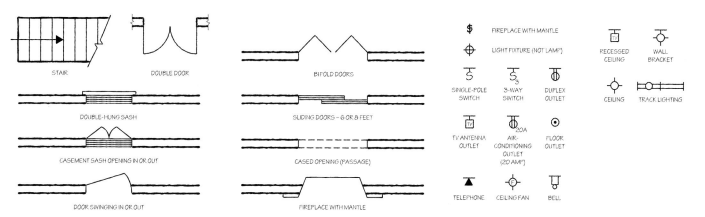

STAIR

DOUBLE DOOR

BIFOLD DOORS

DOUBLE-HUNG SASH

SLIDING DOORS – 6 OR 8 FEET

CASEMENT SASH OPENING IN OR OUT

CASED OPENING (PASSAGE)

DOOR SWINGING IN OR OUT

FIREPLACE WITH MANTLE

FIREPLACE WITH MANTLE

LIGHT FIXTURE (NOT LAMP)

SINGLE-POLE SWITCH

3-WAY SWITCH

DUPLEX OUTLET

TV ANTENNA OUTLET

AIR-CONDITIONING OUTLET (20 AMP)

FLOOR OUTLET

TELEPHONE

CEILING FAN

BELL

RECESSED CEILING

WALL BRACKET

CEILING

TRACK LIGHTING

DINING TABLES AND CHAIRS

Square and Rectangular Tables

Round, Oval, and Shaped Tables

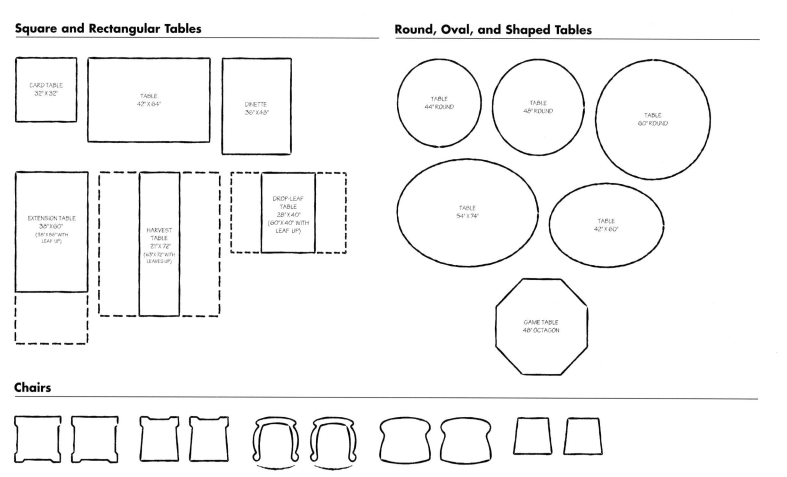

CARD TABLE
32" X 32"

TABLE
42" X 64"

DINETTE
36" X 48"

EXTENSION TABLE
38" X 60"
(38" X 86" WITH LEAF UP)

HARVEST TABLE
21" X 72"
(63" X 72" WITH LEAVES UP)

DROP-LEAF TABLE
28" X 40"
(60" X 40" WITH LEAF UP)

TABLE
44" ROUND

TABLE
48" ROUND

TABLE
60" ROUND

TABLE
54" X 74"

TABLE
42" X 60"

GAME TABLE
48" OCTAGON

Chairs

INTERCHANGEABLE STORAGE AND SPECIAL PIECES

21" Storage

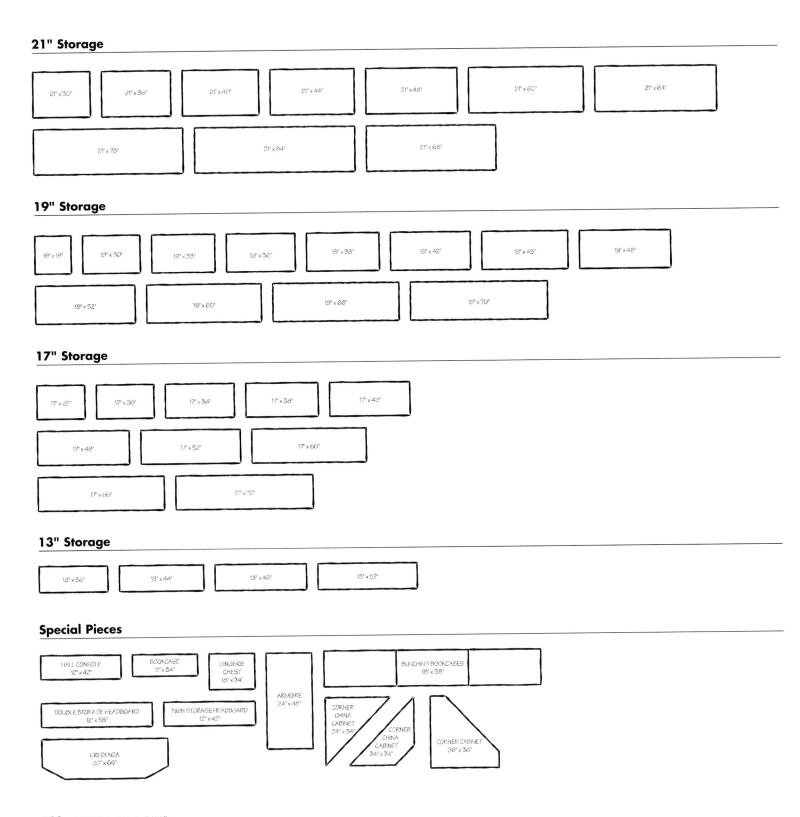

21" x 30" · 21" x 36" · 21" x 40" · 21" x 44" · 21" x 48" · 21" x 60" · 21" x 64"

21" x 78" · 21" x 84" · 21" x 68"

19" Storage

19" x 19" · 19" x 30" · 19" x 33" · 19" x 36" · 19" x 38" · 19" x 42" · 19" x 45" · 19" x 48"

19" x 52" · 19" x 60" · 19" x 66" · 19" x 70"

17" Storage

17" x 25" · 17" x 30" · 17" x 36" · 17" x 38" · 17" x 42"

17" x 48" · 17" x 52" · 17" x 60"

17" x 66" · 17" x 72"

13" Storage

13" x 36" · 13" x 44" · 13" x 48" · 13" x 52"

Special Pieces

HALL CONSOLE 12" x 42" · BOOKCASE 11" x 34" · LINGERIE CHEST 18" x 24" · BUNCHING BOOKCASES 18" x 38"

ARMOIRE 24" x 48"

DOUBLE STORAGE HEADBOARD 12" x 58" · TWIN STORAGE HEADBOARD 12" x 42"

CORNER CHINA CABINET 34" x 34" · CORNER CHINA CABINET 34" x 34" · CORNER CABINET 36" x 36"

CREDENZA 20" x 66"

1 square = 1 square foot

FLOOR PLANS AND STRATEGIES

Rearranging your furniture is the least expensive makeover option of all—and it is the easiest way to give your room a fresh look in as little as an afternoon. This section includes sample floor plans for living rooms, bedrooms, and multipurpose rooms to jump-start your own room makeover as well as tried-and-true strategies for ensuring your rooms can accommodate all the activities you do in them.

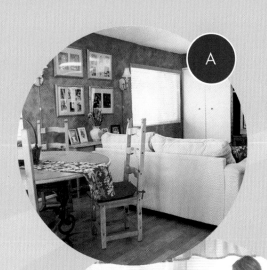

How to Arrange Your Rooms

Prior to moving even a chair, have a plan; use the Room Arranging Kit, beginning on page 178, to map out your new arrangement. Moving large pieces can be tiring, and having a clear plan in mind—and on paper—will eliminate the need to reposition pieces. Also keep the following pointers in mind:

• To gain a better understanding of what new pieces you may need, evaluate what you already have and what activities need to take place in the room (for instance, if you need a desk for computing).

• Keep an eye on traffic flow by eliminating extra furnishings that block easy movement through the room.

• Look beyond furnishings to successfully arrange a room. For instance, choose a living room area rug that is large enough to encompass the seating area; otherwise, it will look like a small island in the middle of the room.

Ⓐ The furnishings in this large room are positioned to create two separate areas: living and dining. Ⓑ Summer puts the finishing touches on a living room/office.

Smart Ideas for Various Shapes of Rooms

Consider these strategies when preparing to rearrange a room:

• Corridor room: A corridor room connects the front entry with the rest of the house. This is most often a living or living/dining room. To ensure traffic flows smoothly around this busy space, position furnishings so that people are encouraged to walk behind or beside the pieces, not through a conversation area.

• L-shape room: Most often, this type of room has an L-shape configuration that wraps around the kitchen. Typically, the short end is used for dining because of its close proximity to the kitchen; the rest of the space is usually a living or family room. While the larger area can accommodate several seating pieces, keeping furnishings to a minimum—and avoiding too many small-scale pieces that can fill up the space—will allow traffic to move easily throughout the room.

• Tunnel room: Living rooms and family rooms with a single entrance are called "tunnel rooms," due to the fact that they appear long and narrow. When all the furnishings line the walls, the "tunnel" is accentuated. To visually widen the space, break up the view with groupings of furniture and place some pieces at angles.

Family Room/Home Office

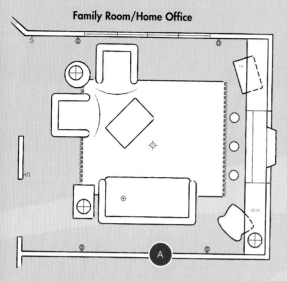

Ⓐ To allow for easy flow around the room, there are minimal furnishings. The furnishings are anchored with an area rug. To usher light into the space, the chairs are placed off-center to the windows. One focal point wall holds the fireplace, TV, and computer. **Ⓑ** The fireplace creates a natural focal point in this room. A conversation grouping is created with large-scale furnishings. A large coffee table bridges that gap between the furnishings, and a sofa table holds lighting and additional accessories to make a visual backdrop for the room.

Living Room 1

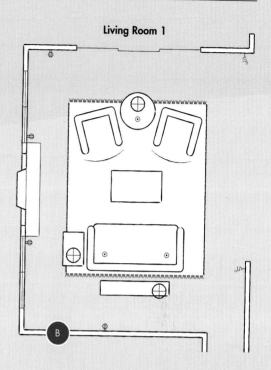

Ⓒ The desk faces into the room; its position also provides views out the window. A small table and two chairs combine for a conversation or meeting area. The bookcases are out of the way, yet near, the desk. **Ⓓ** Small-scale furnishings suit the size of this room. A focal point—a small-scale armoire—is created between the windows. Two benches opposite the love seat provide additional seating An area rug unifies the conversation area.

Home Office

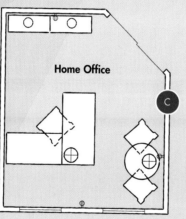

Ⓔ To balance the open floor plan, large-scale furnishings are used. (Smaller furnishings can be incorporated, but they should be grouped to avoid being lost in the large space.) A sectional accommodates multiple people and is positioned to allow for TV viewing or gathering around the fireplace. A small game table with two chairs is tucked behind the sectional; it can be used for playing board games or other activities.

Living Room 2

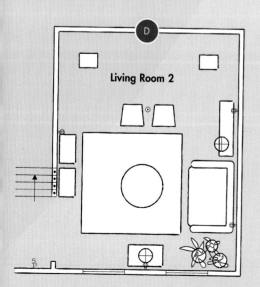

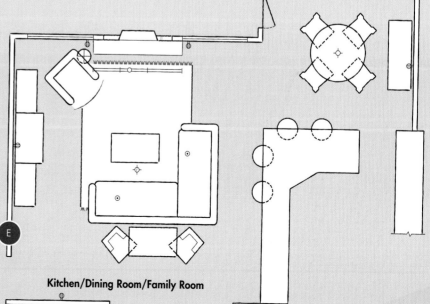

Kitchen/Dining Room/Family Room

A This square room has a large window and a queen-size bed that is just the right size for the space (a king-size would be too large and a full-size too small). Small-scale nightstands anchor the bed. An armoire holds the TV and is positioned to be viewed from the bed, and a small chair angled in the corner can be used for changing footwear and conversation.

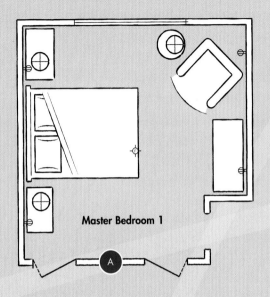

Master Bedroom 1

Child's Bedroom

B One large bed—which faces the door so that it's easy to see who is entering—will easily accommodate a friend or sibling for sleepovers. This room has a large closet, so no dresser is needed. Instead, a low bookcase is used for open storage, and the large nightstand provides additional storage space. A chair positioned near the large window is used for reading or hanging out. Overall, the layout provides ample floor space for various activities.

D This bedroom has twin-size bunk beds in an L position; a dresser can easily be tucked beneath the top bed. A second dresser is placed at the foot of the bed so that each child has individual storage space. Two desks stand side by side in front of the window. Floor pillows allow comfortable seating on the floor. A light is hung by each bed for late-night reading, and other light sources are present throughout the room.

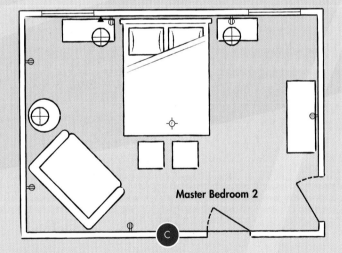

Master Bedroom 2

C This rectangular room has wide windows that allow the large bed to be a focal point. Large-scale nightstands anchor the bed. The two benches at the foot of the bed further establish the bed as a focal point, provide a great place to change footwear, and can easily be moved to become foot rests near a chair. To make this room a getaway, there is ample space for a chair-and-a-half, small chaise, or love seat. An armoire holds the TV and is positioned to be viewed from either the bed or chair. Lighting is evenly balanced throughout the room.

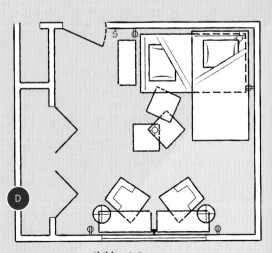

Children's Room

CREDITS ⒶⓃⒹ RESOURCES

Pages 18–25   **Design Team:** Lee Snijders, Summer Baltzer, Charles Burbridge. **Total Project Cost:** $991. **Resources:** Bar counter, Lack, #67298707; legs for riser, Tullsta, #18481; table legs, Curry, #18273; area rug, Faske, #17933; CD holder, Kaxas, #1418: IKEA (www.ikea.com). Rolled vinyl for table, Lg. Coin; colored tiles used as wall art: Linoleum City (www.gtesupersite.com/linoleumcity). Credenza: Nick Metropolis (www.nickmetropolis.com). Shelf brackets for bar/counter, 54455 white: Lowe's (www.lowes.com). Paint, custom color: Behr (www.behr.com).

Pages 26–31   **Design Team:** Sam Kivett, Summer Baltzer, Charles Burbridge. **Total Project Cost:** $997. **Resources:** Love seat, coffee table, end table, buffet lamps: Best Hotel Interiors (323-734-1700). Side chairs, Galvano Technica, 8727C/natural leather: Plummers Furniture (310-837-0138). Burlap, 696237/natural; grommets, 4195665/4195673/silver: JoAnn Fabrics & Crafts (www.joann.com). Sisal rug, Egeby, #18760: IKEA (www.ikea.com). Wall paint, Wild Orchid #2072-40: Benjamin Moore (www.benjaminmoore.com).

Pages 36–43   **Design Team:** Sam Kivett, Summer Baltzer, Charles Burbridge. **Total Project Cost:** $987. **Resources:** Wall paint 1A10-5 Golden Eyes: Behr (www.behr.com). Wing side chair: Play Clothes (818-755-9559). Coffee table: Cort Furniture (www.cort1.com). Wall lights #110500; lampshades #141897 Eggshell; lamp set #133565: Lowe's (www.lowes.com). Picture frames #0000784264 Gold: Aaron Brothers Framing (www.aaronbrothers.com). Decorative urn: Ross Stores (www.rossstores.com). Rug #57492003: Sears (www.sears.com). Window treatments: Kmart (www.bluelight.com).

Pages 46–53   **Design Team:** Sam Kivett, Summer Baltzer, Charles Burbridge. **Total Project Cost:** $989. **Resources:** Bookcases, Billy, 23688010/White; table legs, Curry, 18273/White; tabletop, Amon, 16386/White; chairs, Svante, 13242/White: IKEA (www.ikea.com). Unfinished pine dresser: Jayco Furniture (818-842-3113). Lampshades 202857/White Linen: Lowe's (www.lowes.com). Clip lights 019293290128; table lamp, 082803129409/White: Linens 'n Things (www.linensnthings.com). Base coat paint 1A15-4 Mandarin Mousse (flat) and stripe paint 1A30-4/Gypsy Rose (semi-gloss): Behr (www.behr.com). Dye 048001834804/Tangerine: RIT (www.ritdye.com).

Pages 54–59   **Design Team:** Lee Snijders, Summer Baltzer, Charles Burbridge. **Total Project Cost:** $999. **Resources:** Desktops, 28" interior lauan doors, #10695: Lowe's (ww.w.lowes.com). Bookcases, BCC248412M/Oak: The Barn/Furniture Mart, Inc. (818-785-4253). Rattan armchair, banana leaf: R & R Design Imports (323-231-4347). Cushions: Robert Wylie (323-231-4347). Mosquito netting, Siamcanopy, #718022496076: Linens 'n Things (www.linensnthings.com). Upholstered seat cushion supplies; fabric, Woven Harvest Wheat Beige, #4011035: Foam Mart (818-848-3626). Paint, Classic Burgundy/#1-741: Benjamin Moore (www.benjaminmoore.com). Hanging pendant lights, Hemma cord set, #10175810; desk legs, Curry, #50036501; plastic wastepaper baskets used as shades, Fniss wastepaper basket, #20052012 various colors: IKEA (www.ikea.com).

Pages 62–69   **Design Team:** Sam Kivett, Summer Baltzer, Charles Burbridge. **Total Project Cost:** $997. **Resources:** TV cabinet: Nadeau Imports/Hand Made Furniture Outlet (916-444-3044). Coffee table, Akio, #000000330189; wooden stools, Basni, #00000034640; paper window blinds #000000339038; Chinese takeout containers, #000000046749/Red: Cost Plus (www.costplus.com). Pendant light fixtures, Hemma, #10175810, and Hove, #30017626: IKEA (www.ikea.com). Floor lamp with shade, #11739/tan #19328: Lamps Plus (www.lampsplus.com). Bamboo bale for light fixture and screen: Cane and Basket Supply Co. (www.canebasket.com). Accent pillows: Silk Essence, #1743038/Camel; #1446244/Black; P/C solid #2822419/Ivory; Tailor's Twill, #492470/Camel: JoAnn Fabrics & Crafts (www.joann.com). Paint: dark red, Chestnut 2082-10; dark beige, Dark Beige 2165-40: Benjamin Moore (www.benjaminmoore.com).

Pages 72–79   **Design Team:** Kristan Cunningham, Spencer Anderson, Dave Sheinkopf. **Total Project Cost:** $986. **Resources:** Pine mats for table runner, Sirja #16755: IKEA (www.ikea.com). Wheatgrass mats: Green Set, Inc. (818-764-1231). Vases, #2495862, #2443351: Tuesday Morning (www.tuesdaymorning.com). Glass bowl, #30005; rug, Trocodero: Plummers Furniture (310-837-0138). Chair slipcovers, Dining Slip #067040013: Target (www.target.com). Striped fabric, Stripe Denim Print #6287103: JoAnn Fabrics & Crafts (www.joann.com). Wine cabinet: Design Utopia (323-466-0048). Paint, #082474160121 Interior Flat: Behr (www.behr.com).

Pages 80–85 Design Team: Sam Kivett, Summer Baltzer, Charles Burbridge. **Total Project Cost:** $999. **Resources:** Buffet, Pandan, #1910461; chairs, San Bruno, #1897811: Pier 1 Imports (www.pier1.com). Tab-top sari panels, #40600496305902, tan and blue; curtain rods, #406402407278, silver; plates, #40600496305902, gold; candle globes, #40640770223102, multicolor; plates, #406000155007, flowered; plates, #40600038964802, blue: Ross (www.rossstores.com). Paint, wall, SC16-3, Crown Jewel; screen, #082474350041, Velvet Beige: Behr (www.behr.com).

Pages 86–91 Design Team: Sam Kivett, Summer Baltzer, Charles Burbridge. **Total Project Cost:** $996. **Resources:** Five-piece dining set: Wertz Brothers Furniture (www.wertzbrothers.com). Striped accent fabric: J&P Fabrics (818-845-0862). Tab-top curtains, brushed twill/green: Lowe's (www.lowes.com). Hand-painted bowl and plates: Ross (www.rossstores.com). Photo frames, RAM, #30846: IKEA (www.ikea.com). Track-light kit, #8938241204; bulb covers for fan, #30721815928: Home Depot (www.homedepot.com). Stained-glass spray paint, 3-4510 Yellow, 3-4509 Orange, 3-4506 Red: Mark's Paint Store (818-766-3949). Wall paint, 1A3-3/Chamomile: Behr (www.behr.com).

Pages 92–99 Design Team: Kristan Cunningham, Spencer Anderson, Dave Sheinkopf. **Total Project Cost:** $984. **Resources:** Ladybug fabric, C087; leaf fabric, C968; striped fabric, CC 807; pom-pom fringe for shade, N847: Michael Levine (www.mlfabric.com). Light fixture: White glass 15" FM TX 725916990077: Home Depot (www.homedepot.com). Paint, 082474150122 Interior Flat: Behr (www.behr.com). Couch, Lycksele #30032702; standard mattress, #90032681; couch cover, Lycksele cover natural #0061914; pillow, Red pink orange pillow STRIB CSH #90055069; stuffed animal, Blue Tassa Soft Toy #20057953; orange pillow creature, Krumelur CSH 15: IKEA (www.ikea.com). Table and floor lamps, Corona Bon 1 table/1 sat: Linens 'n Things (www.linensnthings.com). Towel used for pillow, yellow, terrycloth Essence: Target (www.target.com). Round table, A 64699827492; tablecloth, yellow, HE DEC Table A 07200073149: Kmart (www.kmart.com).

Pages 100–105 Design Team: Kristan Cunningham, Spencer Anderson, Dave Sheinkopf. **Total Project Cost:** $999. **Resources:** Green pillow, #96 99195272: The Great Indoors (www.thegreatindoors.com). Pillow fabric: D403 (neckroll); D589: Michael Levine (www.mlfabrics.com). Clock, #65092674: Target (www.target.com). Frame, French Provincial #3300914: The Bombay Company (800-829-7789). Lamp shade for side table lamp, White linen round #202857; closet knobs: Lowe's (www.lowes.com). Lamp shades for fire wood lamps, Shade Seconds, #32847: Lamps Plus (www.lampsplus.com). Window shades, Beige ppr blin #337752: Cost Plus World Market (www.costplus.com). Bench legs, #38453025080; stain for bench legs, #27426227187: The Home Depot (www.homedepot.com). Paint for cornice box trim, Aquavelvet, #2151-50; paint for closet doors and cornice boxes base coat, Moorecraft, #2151-40; wall paint, Moorecraft, #2149-40: Benjamin Moore (www.benjaminmoore.com).

Pages 110–115 Design Team: Sam Kivett, Summer Baltzer, Charles Burbridge. **Total Project Cost:** $990. **Resources:** Bed frame; headboard: Paradise Furnishing (323-469-9702). Bench seat; framed mirror; wall lamps: Best Hotel Interiors (323-734-1700). Unfinished chest of drawers, American Molding, #78860; crackle medium, #96664: Lowe's (www.lowes.com). Fabric, accent pillows, Once and Again, #5914718; drapes, Razi #5835988/Plum; bench cover, Knicknac, #5916523/Lilac: JoAnn Fabrics & Crafts (www.joann.com). Duvet cover, Sateen, #03354024; bed skirt, Sateen, #03354073; drapery rod finials, #09604214822: Linens 'n Things (www.linensnthings.com). Paint, walls, 3B42-2, Subtle Heather; closet doors, 3A34-3, Celestial Plume: Behr (www.behr.com).

Pages 116–121 Design Team: Sam Kivett, Summer Baltzer, Charles Burbridge. **Total Project Cost:** $996. **Resources:** Bookcases, Billy, #40043724; credenza, PS #400351877/white; desk lamps, Expressivo, 00050467/white: IKEA (www.ikea.com). Vintage hubcaps: Culver City Hub Cap (310-559-1200). Wall paint: Water Dance, 1A47-3: Behr (www.behr.com). Vertical blinds: Just Blinds (www.justblinds.com).

Pages 122–127 Design Team: Sam Kivett, Summer Baltzer, Charles Burbridge. **Total Project Cost:** $1,000. **Resources:** Bookcase, Billy, #70023102/medium brown; toy box, Apa, #45510909/natural; dining chairs, Ivar, #68156009/natural; dining table, Lantula, #18217109; floor lamp and shade, Arstid; hanging lamps, Melodi, #20038219; window shades, Bambu, #83508412/natural: IKEA (www.ikea.com). Butcher paper roll, #60746001419: Smart & Final (www.smartandfinal.com). Suede accent pillows on sofa, #4721812451, red: Bed, Bath and Beyond (www.bedbathandbeyond). Picture frames: Aaron Brothers Framing (www.aaronbrothers.com). Paint, 2A1-3, Silk Cypress: Behr (www.behr.com).

Pages 130–135 Design Team: Lee Snijders, Summer Baltzer, Charles Burbridge. **Total Project Cost:** $1,000. **Resources:** Lamps, Orgel, #40018183-15508; bookcases, Billy #93690707-11989: IKEA (www.ikea.com). Paint, #082474130124 Interior Flat: Home Depot (www.homedepot.com). Orchid stems, #1952490; bamboo bundles #1822416 and #1870245: Pier 1 Imports (www.pier1.com). Banana leaf wing chair, TEC 3230: Tien Tong (www.tientong.com). Duvet, #085989305889; sham, #085989305995: Linens 'n Things (www.linensnthings.com). Door knobs, #23384: The Great Indoors (www.thegreatindoors.com).

Pages 136–141 Design Team: Lee Snijders, Summer Baltzer, Charles Burbridge. **Total Project Cost:** $999. **Resources:** Chair pads, #06709164: Target (www.target.com). Kids' table and chair set: Kids Bedroom Center (818-260-9333). Paint, custom mix: Mark's Paint Store (818-766-3949). Copper pot for chandelier, Decorative Giftware #638409: TJ Maxx (www.tjmaxx.com). Lighting, #46622: Lamps Plus (www.lampsplus.com). Photo frames, #45077464027: Michaels Arts & Crafts (www.michaels.com). Throw pillows, #4721837027: Bed Bath and Beyond (www.bedbathandbeyond.com). Console and coffee table: Valley Furniture Store (818-762-2771).

Pages 146–151   **Design Team:** Lee Snijders, Summer Baltzer, Charles Burbridge. **Total Project Cost:** $996.   **Resources:**   Headboard: Hotel Surplus (323-780-7474). Mahogany dresser: Simply Discount Furniture. Chairs: Goodwill Industries. King-size flat sheets, Southgate, #30473941425: Linens 'n Things (www.linensnthings.com). Fabric: Home Fabrics (www.homefabrics.com). Lamps with shades: Target (www.target.com). Curtain rod finials: IKEA (www.ikea.com). Stainless-steel cabinet pulls, #23952: The Great Indoors (www.thegreatindoors.com). Paint, Mellowed Ivory, #2149-50: Benjamin Moore (www.benjaminmoore.com).

Pages 154–159   **Design Team:** Kristan Cunningham, Spencer Anderson, Dave Sheinkopf. **Total Project Cost:** $950.   **Resources:**   Black frames, Regal Black, #415240: Aaron Brothers (www.aaronbrothers.com). Canisters, #2171398413: Bed, Bath and Beyond (www.bedbathandbeyond.com). Vegetable photos: Barry Sheinkopf (www.barrysheinkopf.com). Glaze, Fauxglazeg, #082474748015: The Home Depot (www.homedepot.com). Cloth for mat, Duck 12 oz. Natural 100-percent cotton, NFR Duck012411-Natl lot no. X1: Dazian (www.dazian.com). Pendant light fixtures, Pendant LS O MDSE: The Great Indoors (www.thegreatindoors.com). Cushion fabric, polka dots: Diamond Foam and Fabric (www.diamondfoamandfabric.com). Curtain fabric, burnt orange and gold/orange striped: F&S Fabrics (310-441-2477).

Pages 160–165   **Design Team:** Kristan Cunningham, Spencer Anderson, Dave Sheinkopf. **Total Project Cost:** $997.   **Resources:**   Aluminum table legs, Inge, #90037853; curtains, Gullmaj, #00046625; curtain finials, Deci, #90018637; curtain rod brackets, Deci, #20018631; small picture frames, Ribba, #90019825; lamp, Skyar, #10325310: IKEA (www.ikea.com). Coffee table legs, #98453026650: The Home Depot (www.homedepot.com). Media cabinet, Paler 1A, #328115; side table, TL PSTL Gothic 1A, #340201: Cost Plus World Market (www.costplus.com). Pillows: Boxed Stone, #1816397: Pier 1 Imports (www.pier1.com). Shadow box frames, #689398; clear frames, #84659: Aaron Brothers (www.aaronbrothers.com). Paint, Yorkshire Tan: Benjamin Moore (www.benjaminmoore.com).

Pages 166–171   **Design Team:** Lee Snijders, Summer Baltzer, Charles Burbridge. **Total Project Cost:** $993.   **Resources:**   Chair with ottoman and cushions, Poang CHR, Poang FTST, Poang CHR CSH, Poang FTST CSH, #71003805, #91004205, #71281680, #51281780; metallic gray bookshelves, Billy, #60043723; wall shelving, Rada, #47960783; lighting, Urtima Wall Spotlight, Kassett Light, LANS 7" Shade, #90057191, #00035108, #30036366; glass picture frames, clips, #88046500: IKEA (www.ikea.com). Burgundy duvet cover, #806222043432; burgundy pillow shams, #806222043326; cotton twin navy duvet, #806222043456; cotton standard navy sham, #806222043302: Linens 'n Things (www.linensnthings.com). Putting green supplies: Lowe's (www.lowes.com). Storage containers: Organized Living (www.organizedliving.com). Golf clubs and carry bag, Wilson Irons & Burton Carry Bag, U50120 & U53506: Play It Again Sports (www.playitagainsports.com).

Pages 172-175   **Design Team:** Kristan Cunningham, Spencer Anderson, Dave Sheinkopf. **Total Project Cost:** $999.   **Resources:**   Table lamp, Chimes Table #79891942229; window shade, Redi Shade #75022700237; curtain rod, Cylinder Esprss 28 2783757554; lamp, Chimes Table 79891942229: Bed Bath and Beyond (www.bedbathandbeyond.com). Vintage chair, Nick Metropolis (www.nickmetropolis.com). Headboard pillows, Gosa Lagom Pill; reading lamps, Magiker 90033727: IKEA (www.ikea.com). Headboard aluminum: Lowe's (www.lowes.com). Paint for chair rail, #082474130421 Interior Flat; paint for wall, #082474150122 Interior Flat, #082474160121 Interior Flat: Behr (www.behr.com). Patterned bed pillows, Studio Space #060080342; table, Tele Table #074090149: Target (www.target.com). Window treatment fabric: Diamond Foam and Fabric (www.diamondfoamandfabric.com). Area rug, #302-031 Bamboo Rug: Crate and Barrel (www.crateandbarrel.com). Floating shelf, WDWLL SHLF 2FTDKCH 12-4571287; quilt, MODSTCH QLT FQ CIT 12-4531422: West Elm (www.westelm.com). Orchid, pot: Trader Joe's (www.traderjoes.com).

INDEX